A Strategy for a
Loss of Faith

Marie-Louise von Franz, Honorary Patron

**Studies in Jungian Psychology
by Jungian Analysts**

Daryl Sharp, General Editor

A STRATEGY FOR A LOSS OF FAITH

Jung's Proposal

John P. Dourley

This work was completed through research grant 410-91-0368 from the
Social Science and Humanities Research Council of Canada.

Also by John P. Dourley in this series:
*The Psyche As Sacrament: A Comparative Study of C.G. Jung and
    Paul Tillich* (1981)
The Illness That We Are: A Jungian Critique of Christianity (1984)
Love, Celibacy and the Inner Marriage (1987)

Canadian Cataloguing in Publication Data

Dourley, John P.
 A strategy for a loss of faith

(Studies in Jungian psychology by Jungian analysts; 56)

Includes bibliographical references and index.

ISBN 0-919123-57-0

1. Jung, C.G. (Carl Gustav), 1875-1961 — Views on Christianity.
2. Psychology and religion. 3. Christianity — Controversial literature.
4. Belief and doubt. I. Title. II. Series.

BF51.D68 1992   261.5'15   C92-094356-X

INNER CITY BOOKS
Box 1271, Station Q, Toronto, Canada M4T 2P4
Telephone (416) 927-0355
FAX 416-924-1814

Honorary Patron: Marie-Louise von Franz.
Publisher and General Editor: Daryl Sharp.
Senior Editor: Victoria Cowan.

INNER CITY BOOKS was founded in 1980 to promote the
understanding and practical application of the work of C.G. Jung.

Cover: Ad Parnassum by Paul Klee, 1932. (Kunstmuseum, Berne)

Index by Christopher Blackburn

Printed and bound in Canada by John Deyell Company Limited.

Contents

See final page for other titles by Inner City Books

To A.M.K. for all the good times

Author's Note

The material in this book originated in various addresses to academic bodies for the study of religion and to Jung societies in Canada, the United States, Europe and Australia over the past few years. Some of it has appeared, or will appear, in academic journals. This book, however, stands as a coherent whole and presents an aspect of Jung's psychology that I am far from alone in championing but to which I add a statement not put quite this way by others concerned with much the same issues.

John P. Dourley,
Ottawa, Canada.

1

The Matter with Jung's Father
Is Still the Matter

The substance of Jung's recollection, late in life, of his extended discussion with his minister father over religious matters continues to have enduring interest for religionist, psychologist and those engaged in the fostering of a more adequate contemporary spirituality. Jung's account in his autobiographical *Memories, Dreams, Reflections* is written in a compelling style. The dramatic narrative reads smoothly and soon engages one's own religious positions and sympathies. But there is much at stake in Jung's narrative of his ongoing debate with his father over religion. This is so because Jung's description of the psychological difficulties his father's religion posed to his father's fuller development as a human being relates closely and consistently to Jung's more measured critique of Christianity throughout his work.

Jung's diagnosis of the pathologizing features of his father's religiosity uncovers more than a personal eccentricity peculiar to a single individual unhappily but atypically victimized by his religion. Rather, when related to Jung's total work, his analysis of his father's personal religious difficulties reveals them to be a microcosm of the current pathology of Christian consciousness on a macrocosmic scale. Read in this light the matter with Jung's father remains the matter with much of Christianity.

In this context Jung's analysis does two things. It reveals the issues at stake in his dialogue with his father to be lifelong impelling forces in the formulation of Jung's mature psychology, and it strongly suggests that those still influenced by Christianity are forced by its limitations to continue to grapple with the problems encountered by his father. The deeper question is to what extent Christianity could divest itself of those characteristics which so pathologized Jung's father and still remain itself. Or are his father's difficulties themselves powerful indicators that a supplanting myth is currently needed and in the process of being born, a myth to which Jung's psychology makes a significant contribution?

At the heart of his father's problem, as Jung saw it, is the threat his father's religious perspective posed to the personal and social development of its holder's fuller humanity. At the societal level the implications of Jung's father's faith pose a threat to human survival in so much as such faith is based on the literalist conception of a monotheistic and wholly transcendent God working a final revelation through an historical figure whose resultant community then becomes the chosen or favored of God. Believers in this final revelation, one among a number, cannot seriously relativize let alone surpass it. Western history shows clearly that unqualified claims to religious ultimacy cannot tolerate competing claims. As a consequence the historical culmination of the final revelation in the final solution has become all too evident, indeed systemically necessary, though members of the faith communities involved as perpetrators and victims seem still largely incapable of making the connection between the revelations themselves and their dubious outcome.

At the individual level, as documented by Jung in *Memories, Dreams, Reflections*, such faith is no less destructive. Jung came to see that the faith of his father disconnects its holder from fuller access to the life-giving energies of the psyche by locating divinity beyond the psyche, to be accessed only in relatively pallid projection. In many cases the dim and distant energies ecclesially mediated leave the believer, as in the case of Jung's father, in varying states of mild depression or worse, rather far removed from the promised good news of life in abundance.

Jung's problems with his father's religiosity as it worked to deny his father's maturity appear in *Memories, Dreams, Reflections* in the same temporal sequence as the book itself is written. This is hardly noteworthy in an autobiography. But isolation of the texts in which Jung dwells on his relationship to his father have a crescendo effect on the reader. Such an effect lends considerable support to Jung's implication that his "Answer to Job"[1] is to a great extent the outcome of his struggle with his father and his father's religion. When viewed as reactive to his father's religion, Jung's psychology appears more clearly as a full-blown countermyth creatively surpassing the myth that so constricted his father's life and could so easily have maimed his own. His psychological work becomes then a sustained effort to heal the wound his father's kind of religion inflicted on his father and, by extension, on individual and society to the extent they con-

---

1. *Psychology and Religion*, CW 11, pp. 355ff. [CW refers throughout to *The Collected Works of C.G. Jung* (Bollingen Series XX), 20 vols., trans. R.F.C. Hull, ed. H. Read, M. Fordham, G. Adler, Wm. McGuire; Princeton: Princeton University Press, 1953-1979]

tinue to be victimized by the devastating effects of a similar religiosity.

What follows is an examination of the major themes in Jung's recall of his relation to his father over religious matters.

Jung's account of the father-mother relation

Jung's earliest recorded memories of his father are those of an infant consoled by his father's voice, "singing over me in the stillness of the night."[2] This positive note is never wholly absent whenever he mentions his father in his autobiography. Yet for Jung his father's tenderness, conscious good intentions and compassion carried with them a certain ambiguity which somehow combined "reliability and—powerlessness."[3] Jung later amplifies what he means by this strange combination: "He did a great deal of good—far too much—and as a result was usually irritable."[4]

Reading these lines from the viewpoint of Jung's understanding of the male shadow, he is here depicting in his father a man unable to allow his shadow into his conscious life. Probably Jung's father could not do so because of the collective persona projected onto a parson and his family by his flock and too often accepted by its recipients. Those burdened with such a persona must accept the demand of their congregation for a public and private perfection incompatible with healthy psychological development. Efforts to live up to this projection by living a stainless life in the footsteps of the central figure in the Christian myth might well account for his father's residual irritability. Holier than the saints are those who must live with them. Such efforts to be a perfect Christian may also account for some of the difficulties with his wife. Jung points out she too sought to lead a devout Christian life, though with his mother a gifted native resonance with the unconscious may have spared her the more severe consequences of such devotion.[5]

It is not difficult to establish that children growing up in an environment of expected perfection frequently become its victims. Too much of their shadow is early on suppressed and later life comes largely to be a continuation of this suppression. Within the Reform tradition the "preacher's kid"

---

2. *Memories, Dreams, Reflections*, ed. Aniela Jaffe (New York: Vintage Books, 1961), p. 8.
3. Ibid.
4. Ibid., p. 91.
5. Ibid., pp. 91-92.

syndrome is so widespread that it has become almost a clinical category. Jung's psychology has brought the theological roots of such pathology— an inhumane moralism, enforced by theological doctrines of the sinfulness of humanity—closer to diagnostic identification and treatment.

Nor does current Christian pathology belong entirely to that Reformed Christianity in which Jung so clearly identified it. Roman Catholicism continues to impose celibacy on its all-male leadership, contributing to an increasingly large homoerotic component in such leadership. The insistence on non-optional celibacy thus effectively produces a growing gay environment in the priesthood. This sociological shift, even if artificially induced, may add much to the quality of the priesthood since gay psychology is unquestionably deeply spiritual. But there is a tension bordering on hypocrisy to continue questioning the morality of homosexuality while effectively building so much of the future priesthood upon it. On the other hand, psychosexual immaturity in the Roman priestly caste is increasingly evident in the media and courts in the form of pedophilia, compelling evidence of the truncated development of the heterosexual psyche within this environment.

The perplexed onlooker is faced with the dark mystery that Christian communities that allow their leaders to procreate not infrequently inflict great damage on their offspring, while Christian communities which deny procreation can inflict equally great damage on their leadership and through the leadership on their parishioners. The situation raises the paradox that the possibility of escaping damage to oneself or to one's family would appear slight among those most dedicated to the good news. In the face of this, one has the feeling that the myth itself is somehow currently dehumanizing and has lost a wholesomeness that only a recovery of a deeper, God-grounded humanity can restore.

As noted, Jung's psychology has been an important contributor to the identification of the theological roots of such pathologies. Assisted by a Jungian sensitivity, the therapeutic world may be on the brink of identifying adult children of believing Christians as the first step toward helping them.

Jung's contribution to the program for the recovering Christian would have to be founded on the principle that the God who talks directly to the pathologically unbalanced from the unconscious and through the dream is a God whose intent is human wholeness as the only expression in which divinity is real. Other deities and their historical spokesmen who would place perfection before totality are for Jung the enemies of individual and collective humanity. Jung may have had such pathologizing perfectionism, the enemy of wholeness, in mind when he wrote, perhaps with a touch of irony, "The Christ-image fully corresponds to this situation: Christ is the perfect man who is crucified. One could hardly think of a truer picture of the goal of ethical endeavour."[6] Jung's point here, as throughout his work, is hardly inimical to ethical endeavor since his psychology contains in itself a most rigorous ethic and ascetic. Rather this citation is a caustic comment on the way in which the search for "perfection" can truncate a broader human spirit and needs itself to be crucified.

Jung's memory of his father singing to him in the night is associated on the same page with Jung's equally early recall of the trouble between his parents and an early period of separation from his mother due to her hospitalization.[7] When *Memories, Dreams, Reflections* is read in the context of Jung's wider work, one can again use Jung's own psychology to identify the archetypal basis of his parents' conflict.

Jung's mother provided one of his earliest accesses to that dimension of psychic life he was later to call the collective unconscious.[8] At times she could speak to Jung's personality number two, that side of himself grounded in eternity even while personality number one lived within the limitations of life in this world of time, space and finitude. For Jung this meant that his mother herself was in living touch with this realm, indeed, could on occasion speak out of it and so lead him into it. Her native contact with these depths Jung called her natural mind, "ruthless as truth and nature."[9] These naturally pagan, that is deeply human, vitalities so readily available to his mother remained foreign to his father's Christian consciousness, which imprisoned him in the lifeless rationalism of what Jung was to term the now "sacrosanct unintelligibility"[10] of its religious and theological formulations.

An examination of his father's Christian entrapment in the world of consciousness, from the perspective of the son's mature psychology,

---

6. "Christ, A Symbol of the Self," *Aion*, CW 9ii, par. 124.
7. *Memories, Dreams, Reflections*, p. 8.
8. Ibid., pp. 48-52.
9. Ibid., p. 50. See also p. 90 where Jung associates his mother's psyche with pagan, in distinction from Christian, sensitivities.
10. "A Psychological Approach to the Dogma of the Trinity," *Psychology and Religion*, CW 11, par. 170.

would point to a pathology derived from his father's removal by his religion itself from the vital energies of the unconscious. From Jung's mature perspective the numinous power of the unconscious creates religious experience, and institutionalized religion, based on these experiences, serves and mediates them.

His father's consciousness as uprooted in the name of religion from the origin of religion in the unconscious perfectly illustrates the somewhat technical meaning Jung was to give to patriarchy. For Jung the term describes the pathologized consciousness of members of either gender when their conscious mind is severed from its roots in the archetypal and so divested of the experience of humanity's native divinity. States of consciousness such as Jung attributes to his father, though well intentioned, understandably produce the irritability and sometimes rage alternating with depression common to males divorced from the anima, the feminine power in the male psyche. This cuts them off from the enabling energies of the Goddess, which are mediated by the anima.

In stark contrast to his father, Jung describes his mother as more firmly grounded in her humanity. He writes, "She always seemed to me the stronger of the two. Nevertheless I always felt on her side when my father gave vent to his moody irritability."[11] Thus Jung grew up in a home environment in which the split between the unconscious and the conscious, a split he identified as the major blight in his culture, was incarnate in his parents. His mother's natural resonance with the unconscious, and her familiarity with the natural mind, remained forever foreign to his father and to the shallower religious sensitivity of the patriarchal mind.

It was not surprising, then, that the split evident in his parents' differing psychologies became increasingly evident to Jung in collective religion and culture. His religion's reduction of his father's wider personality to consciousness both reflected and provided the sacred basis for society's continued deification of reason, especially technical reason bent on the exploitation of all realms of nature including the human. Faced with such opposites in his parents and in society Jung came to place greater value on his mother's groundedness in the unconscious. Indeed he came to see the rerooting of individual and society in these deeper and natively religious levels of the psyche as the only significant and radical resource in healing the patriarchal suffering of contemporary culture.

---

11. *Memories, Dreams, Reflections*, p. 25.

In this dimension of his cultural critique and in the hope that informed it, Jung may have been naive, at least in regard to institutional Christianity. For the recognition by mainstream Western institutional religions and their supporting theologies that they are products of the religious impulse emanating from the unconscious, and exist to serve this impulse, remains as foreign to such institutions in today's world as it was to the institution his father served.

The absence in Jung's father's faith of a foundation in immediate experience

Jung's critique of this aspect of his father's faith was at the core of their difficulties and extended over the years of their conversations on religion. At the heart of the conflict lies Jung's claim to an early, continued and ready access to the world of the unconscious as the basis of an endemic appreciation of religion as immediate experience.

Over against the son's natural religiosity stood his father's near total removal from any religious sensitivity grounded in his human nature. Rather his father's religion was anchored in an intellectual adherence in faith to doctrinal assertions whose meaning, the elder Jung confessed to his son, were largely unintelligible to him. Such was his reply to his son's curiosity about the doctrine of the Trinity on the occasion of his preparation by his father for confirmation. Jung had anticipated with some eagerness his father's addressing the intriguing mystery of the Trinity, and so was understandably disappointed when his father dismissed the discussion in these terms, "We come to the Trinity, but we'll skip that, for I really understand nothing of it myself."[12] For Jung this reply was an early and abiding indication of the split between human experience and faith which made of the latter something foreign to the humanity it allegedly enlivened.

Jung's experience of the unconscious, which he was later to identify as the matrix of archetypal and so of religious experience, began early in life. At the age of four he dreamt of the enthroned phallus beneath his father's vicarage.[13] One might ask of the dream, in terms of Jung's own later theory of compensation, what compensation it might proffer to a four year old? One might answer, again in terms of Jungian dream theory, that the

12. Ibid., p. 53.
13. Ibid., pp. 11-12.

dream was prospective in the sense that it functioned as a premonitory revelation of his adult vocation. This vocation was to reveal the divinities of the underworld to a too-conscious Christianity and culture unable to admit the reality and power of the darker sides of the divine and so destined to suffer from their unwanted invasions.

Of all these early experiences of the natural religious power of the unconscious, the adolescent anxiety which culminated in the image of divinity destroying its own cathedral at Basel seems to have been one which set the tone for much of Jung's later reflection on the relation of humanity to God and of both to the psyche. As a youth of twelve, after a willed recovery from an admitted childhood neurosis which could have taken him out of life,[14] Jung was haunted by the sense that something demanded entrance to his consciousness which his consciousness could ill receive. In part his adolescent ruminations centered around the mystery of evil and creation. Under such stress he came to some preliminary insight that the birth of consciousness and expulsion of Adam and Eve from the garden of Eden were very closely related. Here lay the more remote origins of a very modern and now more widespread realization even in theological circles, namely, that the original sin repeated in each life is the will to be conscious as disobedience to the divine decree to remain unconscious.

It was against the background of such agitated rumination that his second youthful revelation came. When Jung could no longer resist and "let the thought come," it was this: "God sits on His golden throne, high above the world—and from under the throne an enormous turd falls upon the sparkling new roof, shatters it, and breaks the walls of the cathedral."[15] Allowing this image entry to consciousness was for Jung an experience of "enormous [and] indescribable relief . . . the miracle of grace."[16]

This experience came to mean many things for Jung. In the first instance he took it to be an immediate experience of God as a freeing power accessed not in some external heaven nor through earthly institutions, but as a power rising to meet him from the depths of his own life. This immediate and experiential access to God in and through human interiority came to be the seminal difference between his understanding of religion and his father's. Jung expresses it in these words:

---

14. Ibid., pp. 30-31.
15. Ibid., p. 39.
16. Ibid., p. 40.

That was what my father had not understood, I thought; he had failed to experience the will of God, had opposed it for the best reasons and out of the deepest faith. And that was why he had never experienced the miracle of grace which heals all and makes all comprehensible. He had taken the Bible's commandments as his guide; he believed in God as the Bible prescribed and as his forefathers had taught him. But he did not know the immediate living God who stands, omnipotent and free, above His Bible and His Church, who calls upon man to partake of His freedom, and can force him to renounce his own views and convictions in order to fulfill without reserve the command of God.[17]

Yet what Jung was to call his "secret," his immediate experience of God freeing him from bible, church and meaningless dogma, remained unexperienced and unappreciated in the ecclesial and spiritual atmosphere of his youth. Such spiritual obtuseness caused Jung considerable perplexity and suffering. He writes of the strange paradox he saw around him that religious experience should remain so foreign to those whose profession was its dissemination:

In my mother's family there were six parsons, and on my father's side not only was my father a parson but two of my uncles also. Thus I heard many religious conversations, theological discussions and sermons. Whenever I listened to them I had the feeling: "Yes, yes, that is all very well. But what about the secret? The secret is also the secret of grace. None of you know anything about that. You don't know that God wants to force me to do wrong, that he forces me to think abominations in order to experience His grace.[18]

Jung adds that he found no resonance with the secret of his native experience of the divine, and the questions it raised about the divine-human relation, in his early forays into works of theology.[19] Orthodox theological descriptions of God appeared even to the youthful Jung as transparently anthropomorphic. Whenever he tried to argue with his father that experience should be the basis of faith and not its opposite, he met with simple incomprehension. Nor was all the difficulty on the part of the father. Jung assumes some responsibility for the failure of their dialogue when he admits that as a young man he could not help his father because their conver-

17. Ibid.
18. Ibid., p. 42.
19. Ibid.

sations were too conscious, too much in Jung's thinking function. Of the impasse and the frustration he experienced in not being able to get through to his father, Jung writes, "What he said sounded stale and hollow, like a tale told by someone who knows it only by hearsay and cannot quite believe it himself. I wanted to help him, but I did not know how."[20]

Thus the son could not help the father connect with his own religious depths. Moreover, Jung began to see that his father, divested of any immediate experience, could only participate in theological discussion as an all too predictable representative of theological orthodoxy, a cadre of the dogmatic party line. He confesses, "I would have liked to lay my religious difficulties before him and ask him for advice, but I did not do so because it seemed to me that I knew in advance what he would be obliged to reply out of his respect for his office."[21] Jung could not break through this faith-induced insensitivity to religious experience that separated them. He describes the mutual exasperation engendered by their discussions:

> They irritated him, and saddened him. "Oh nonsense," he was in the habit of saying, "you always want to think. One ought not to think, but believe." I would think, "No, one must experience and know," but I would say "Give me this belief," whereupon he would turn resignedly away.[22]

The absence of any connection of faith with the immediate experience of God became for Jung a form of spiritual death that pervaded both the Church and those like his father caught up in its lethal faith consciousness. He writes of his perception of the religious tragedy of his father's ecclesial and personal faith in forceful terms:

> "Why, that is not religion at all," I thought. "It is an absence of God; the church is a place I should not go to. It is not life which is there but death."
> I was seized with the most vehement pity for my father. All at once I understood the tragedy of his profession and his life. He was struggling with a death whose existence he could not admit. An abyss had opened between him and me, and I saw no possibility of ever bridging it, for it was infinite in extent. I could not plunge my dear and generous father, who in so many matters left me to myself and had never tyrannized over me, into that despair and sacrilege which were necessary for an experience of divine grace.[23]

---

20. Ibid., p. 43.
21. Ibid., p. 52.
22. Ibid., p. 43.
23. Ibid., p. 55.

As Jung reflected on the psychological consequences of his father's faith, he came to understand that much of his father's energies were wasted in suppressing the doubts that inevitably accompany a faith divested of a grounding in one's total human nature. This side of his father's pathology is again frequently seen in the contemporary believer and clergy. Doubts must be suppressed along with the unconscious lest dialogue with it threaten one's faith. The paradox of this side of ecclesial pathology is that one must remain unconscious to function comfortably in a ministerial or priestly role, as well as in the role of devotee. Of this aspect of his father's suffering Jung writes:

> Not until several years later did I come to understand that my poor father did not dare to think, because he was consumed by inward doubts. He was taking refuge from himself and therefore insisted on blind faith. He could not receive it as a grace because he wanted to "win it by struggle," forcing it to come with convulsive efforts.[24]

These doubts to which, claims Jung, his father was later to succumb, produced "shadows . . . all the longer the more my father's conscious mind resisted their power."[25] No doubt much of his father's irritability stemmed from his efforts to repress such doubts and the wider, life-giving empathy and perspective the doubts themselves might release from the unconscious through the anima if their forbidden vitalities were allowed to surface into consciousness.

With so much energy devoted to the suppression of life in the name of faith, it is little wonder that Jung depicts his father as having shown his true self only once in his maturity. The occasion was at a student gathering when his father let himself regress, as it were, to the more spontaneous life he had led as a student, free from the later constrictive persona of the parson. When Jung saw this side of his father,

> I realized in a flash that his life had come to a standstill at his graduation. . . . The speech he delivered that summer evening over the wine was the last chance he had to live out his memories of the time when he was what he should have been."[26]

His father died the following year.

Thus for Jung the central mystery of his father's life as a minister was

---

24. Ibid., p. 73.
25. Ibid., p. 90.
26. Ibid., p. 95.

that he remained insensitive to the immediate experience of God at the heart of all religion. Paradoxically this experience was readily available to Jung, the developing doctor and psychologist, and not to his father, the servant of a community allegedly built on such experience and dedicated to it. On this contradiction Jung writes:

> It appeared almost inconceivable to me that he should not have had experience of God, the most evident of all experiences. I knew enough about epistemology to realize that knowledge of this sort could not be proved, but it was equally clear to me that it stood in no more need of proof than the beauty of the sunset or the terrors of the night.[27]

When Jung states that the experience of God is "the most evident of all experiences," he should be taken seriously because, in less candid manner, the sentiment informs much of his understanding of the psyche and his psychology. In these passages Jung goes on to say that, through his experience of the unconscious, God had allowed him "a glimpse into His own being."[28] The metaphysical implications of this statement should not be taken lightly. Jung here enters the ontological-epistemological domain and in his *Collected Works* unmistakably attributes religious experience as such to unconscious activity and its impact on consciousness.[29] In this late and poetic formulation Jung may reveal the full force of what he intimates so consistently throughout his work, that the psyche itself provides the attentive observer with a glimpse of the divine.

But Jung's most cherished secret, his glimpse of the divine being, found no response in his father who remained incapable of understanding the direct experience of God. Such religious insensitivity became for Jung the sin faith committed against humanity. He writes, "The arch sin of faith, it seemed to me, was that it forestalled experience."[30] Victims of such faith were condemned "to believe . . . without hope. This is what my father had tried valiantly to do, and had run aground."[31] Jung could never accept this

---

27. Ibid., p. 92.
28. Ibid., p. 28.
29. This is nowhere more explicit than when Jung writes, "It is a telling fact that two theological reviewers of my book *Psychology and Religion*—one of them Catholic, the other Protestant—assiduously overlooked my demonstration of the psychic origin of religious phenomena." ("Introduction to the Religious and Psychological Problems of Alchemy," *Psychology and Alchemy,* CW 12, par. 9)
30. *Memories, Dreams, Reflections,* p. 94.
31. Ibid.

conception of the life of faith divested of hope and, he might well have added, of that joy that flows to consciousness from the experience of that point of intersection of divinity and humanity.

It is not surprising then that Jung came increasingly to view his father's faith as a drain on his father's energy and as a betrayal of his fuller humanity. His anger is evident when he recalls,

> Once I heard him praying. He struggled desperately to keep his faith. I was shaken and outraged at once, because I saw how hopelessly he was entrapped by the Church and its theological thinking. They had blocked all avenues by which he might have reached God directly, and then faithlessly abandoned him.[32]

Jung is succinct and dramatic when he restates his father's religious dilemma, the conflict between the spirit of his faith and the spirit of his humanity, in these terms, "He wanted to rest content with faith but faith broke faith with him."[33] Such faith as constraining a fuller humanity is the faith Jung identifies with psycho-spiritual death. It is not surprising then that as his dialogue with his father continued and the issues became more clearly defined, Jung was compelled to reject his father's theology of faith in the interests of the survival of his own spirit. He writes, "Theology had alienated my father and me from one another."[34]

Thus Jung parted company with his father over the issue of faith as experiential. But the very experiences that convinced Jung that faith was experiential also gave a different substance to his faith, a substance his father's faith could hardly assimilate. As stated, the vision that came to attach to Jung's understanding of faith implied the necessity of the sin of consciousness in the process of human maturation. It further implied that divinity sought not only its consciousness but also the resolution of its own self-contradiction in the historical consciousness of humanity. This cosmology involved humanity and divinity in an organic process of mutual redemption of so intimate a nature that the true partnership of human and divine became much more than a pious proclamation.

All of these consequences were to follow from Jung's sustained reflection on the image of the divine defecation on the cathedral at Basle. Jung writes, "God in His omniscience had arranged everything so that the first

---

32. Ibid., p. 93.
33. Ibid., p. 215.
34. Ibid., p. 93.

parents would have to sin. *Therefore it was God's intention that they should sin.*[35] This insight is foundational to the making of Jung's own myth which counters that of his father's and in his maturity worked an appreciative undermining of it.

The shift to the quaternity and the ultimate incompatibility between Jung and his father on the nature of religion

We have just heard Jung state that through his personal religious experience he became convinced that God drove the developing human to sin. The sin that God demanded of the creature, even as he forbade it, was the sin of consciousness.

As this insight developed, helped both by his reaction to his father and to his father's appearances in later dreams, Jung came to the conclusion that the divine-human relation would be better imaged in the myth of an eternally conflicted God forced to create human consciousness in order to become conscious and so find redemption in it. This pillar of Jung's mature work quite clearly gives to human consciousness a certain discriminatory superiority to its divine matrix, even as consciousness remains dependent on its precedent and fearfully respectful of it in the maturational process.

This radical shift of religious perspective is made explicit in Jung's understanding of the last two dreams in which his father appeared, as recounted in *Memories, Dreams, Reflections.* Jung introduces this dream material with the remark that he was helped in his research and its quest by his own dreams throughout his life. He suggests that this was especially the case in his mature work on alchemy and on its central theme of the *coniunctio,* understood in its broadest terms as the union of consciousness with the unconscious in the birth of the Self. It is in this context of the contribution that they made to his understanding of the psyche and of the divine-human relation implicit in this understanding that Jung introduces the two late dreams about his father.

Leading into the first of these, Jung writes that "both this [the alchemical *coniunctio*] and the Christ problem were condensed in a remarkable image."[36] One understands why the dream and its image was so remark-

---

35. Ibid., p. 38.
36. Ibid., p. 213.

able when one examines the dream text. In it Jung enters a wing of his house unknown to himself and discovers his father's laboratory filled with specimens of fish. Though absent personally in the dream, his dream father was obviously studying ichthyology! Jung interprets this part of the dream to point to the continued importance for both the dream father and so for Jung, the dreamer, of the Christ figure, frequently symbolized by the fish.[37]

As the dream continues a strong wind is felt. A young rustic man, Hans, appears and Jung asks him if a window is open. He investigates and returns terrified, reporting that he had discovered a part of the house was haunted. When Jung pushed into this room he found where his mother lived. From its walls were suspended five small garden pavilions, each with two beds in which ghostly couples lived. Apparently his mother had set up these pavilions for these strange couples. Opposite his mother's room was another room where a brass band played in what looked like a hotel lobby.

Jung took the juxtaposition of rooms and the dramatically different ambience attaching to each to point behind the façade of superficial everyday jollity, the brass band, to the world of the unconscious and the power of its Spirits. As he continues his amplification Jung associates the room of his mother where ghostly couples are accommodated with the *coniunctio*, the unity of opposites here sexually depicted.

Jung took the overall thrust of the dream to mean that both his mother and father in different ways were faced with the cure of their souls from the suffering imposed on them by their Christianity, symbolized in his father's continued interest in fish. By the fact that they appeared in his dream, Jung understood that the problem had remained unsolved in his parents' lives and so asked for resolution in his own. This remark is but a variant on Jung's wider theme that each age is faced with the solution of its problems which, if left unresolved, become then a form of psycho-historical karma for subsequent generations. Read in this light, the dream would make the problem his Christian parents had failed to solve Jung's own. Even late in life his unconscious was insisting he "had not answered the question which the Christian soul put to me."[38]

As he continues his amplification of this dream, Jung dwells more on

---

37. Ibid., pp. 213-214.
38. Ibid., pp. 214-215.

his father's problematic situation than on his mother's. He identifies his father's suffering with the wound of the fisher king Amfortas, inflicted by his Christianity. In so doing he again makes of his father's suffering a microcosm of the suffering inflicted on the Christian by Christianity, whose healing was the goal of the alchemical search for the grail. This could hardly be put more explicitly than when Jung writes:

> My memory of my father is of a sufferer stricken with an Amfortas wound, a "fisher king" whose wound would not heal—that Christian suffering for which the alchemists sought the panacea. I as a "dumb" Parsifal was the witness of this sickness during the years of my boyhood, and, like Parsifal, speech failed me . . . his suffering . . . [was] the suffering of the Christian in general.[39]

Even though at the time of this dream Jung had already completed his work on gnosticism and the intimacy it establishes between the divine and the human *(Aion,* CW 9ii), the dream pressed him yet further. In commenting on the dream's challenge to take up the cure of the Christian soul, Jung had to admit that at the time he had neither the insight, nor, in a certain sense, the courage, to overcome his remaining resistance to what was to surface later: "I still had to overcome the greatest inner resistances before I could write *Answer to Job.*"[40]

By his own admission he was helped in overcoming this resistance by a second late dream in which his father played a major role.[41] In this dream his father is portrayed as living a rural life at a former country inn. He was guardian of the sarcophagi of famous people and princes. He was also a distinguished scholar, a tribute, notes Jung, never paid to his father throughout his career. In the presence of two mutual acquaintances, a father and son, both psychiatrists, his father began an interpretation of a passage from the Pentateuch, using a Bible bound in fish skin. His father's interpretation was made so swiftly and with such intensity that it went over the heads of his three listeners and even provoked the laughter of the younger psychiatrist.

In his interpretation of this dream Jung sees in his father his own shadow still deeply involved with the archetypal truth of the scriptures, but unable to communicate with his other shadow side represented by two

---

39. Ibid., p. 215.
40. Ibid., p. 216.
41. Ibid., pp. 217f.

generations of psychiatrists, whom Jung describes as "in part incapable of understanding, in part maliciously stupid."[42]

Having established the fact that Jung's interest in the contemporary religious-cultural problem still bubbled on within him, imaged in his dream father's continued engagement with Scripture in tension with science, the dream shifts venue to make its most telling point and, in Jung's estimate, to provide him with the key to his answer to Job or Job's answer to Yahweh. The dream moves into a room shaped like a mandala. There a sultan presides from an elevated seat in the center, surrounded by his court in a gallery running around the higher ceiling. Then Jung saw in the dream that from the center another set of stairs ascended to a spot high up on the wall where there was a small door. His father said, "Now I will lead you into the highest presence," and proceeded to kneel and touch his forehead to the floor. Jung also knelt but could not bring himself to touch his forehead to the floor. Moreover, he suddenly knew that the person in the holy of holies to whom his father bowed was Uriah.[43]

Jung's dream refusal to worship Uriah thus imaged a refusal to become a second Uriah in the service of a God or his representative, David, who had betrayed the loyalty of his servant. We have heard Jung say that his father's faith in the God he worshipped had betrayed his father's loyalty by betraying his humanity. The dream suggests that Jung had seen through such faith in such a God and so had rejected a total act of faith in the God who had betrayed and corroded his father's masculinity and humanity. Among other implications of the dream, Jung felt it fated him to expose publicly, in what came to be his *Answer to Job,* "God's tragic contradictoriness," whose resolution was humanity's task.[44]

All of these implications are drawn out when Jung amplifies the meaning of his refusal to touch his forehead to the floor before Uriah. It would deny humanity's conscious superiority to divinity, even if by only the millimeter which separated Jung's forehead from the floor. Jung comments, "Man always has some mental reservation, even in the face of divine decrees. Otherwise, where would be his freedom? And what would be the use of that freedom if it could not threaten Him who threatens it?"[45]

The full implication of the dream, developed in his *Answer to Job* and

42. Ibid., p. 219.
43. Ibid.
44. Ibid., p. 216. See also p. 220.
45. Ibid., p. 220.

in his mature psychology, is that it "discloses a thought and a premonition that have long been present in humanity: the idea of the creature that surpasses its creator by a small but decisive factor."[46] Thus the dream points to the creator's need to create human consciousness as the suffering theater of history, where alone the creation of sin and the sin of creation can be resolved. Jung summarizes his psycho-theology of creation, his Christology and his understanding of redemption when he writes, "This leads inescapably to the question: Who is responsible for these sins? In the final analysis it is God who created the world and its sins, and who therefore became Christ in order to suffer the fate of humanity."[47]

Since Jung claims that these dreams helped him in his formulation of the position he took in *Answer to Job,* here imaged as a myth healing the Christian wound, let us conclude with a brief systematic analysis of that work and its religious implications. Presenting its contents systematically both is and is not an imposition on the work. The work is of an unusual genre. It is written with the contracted intensity of a piece of poetry. It obviously speaks, indeed screams, in symbolic outburst. Jung describes the work as written "in the form in which the problem had presented itself to me, that is, as an experience charged with emotion."[48] At the same time it could be viewed as Jung's *Summa,* because it is one of his most precisely systematic expositions of the archetypal psyche and of its religion-making propensity as it impacts on individual and historical consciousness. In it he brings to explicit formulation the fruit of his reflection on religion born in no small part from his differences with his father in earthly and dream dialogue. As such the work can be viewed as Jung's countermyth which appreciates even as it corrodes that of his father.

Yahweh, the God of this work, is not the Trinitarian God of Christianity who unites from all eternity the opposing forces of divine life as the precondition of creation. Rather the God Job faces is beset with inner contradictions He cannot resolve within the supposedly eternally integrated process of His life. As Jung continues his meditation from this point of departure he cannot escape the conclusion that divine life creates human consciousness as the sole point of conscious discrimination in existence. This paradigm makes humanity the fourth element in the Trinity. Only through human discrimination can a badly conflicted Yahweh first perceive

---

46. Ibid.
47. Ibid., p. 216.
48. Ibid., p. 217.

the living self-contradiction or antinomy that He is.

Job, for Jung, represents that stage of religious historical development in which human consciousness comes to realize that it is an inevitable consequence of divine self-contradiction and that this contradiction seeks its resolution in humanity because there is none in divinity. In his confrontation with Job, the insight Yahweh gains of his own volatile instability shames Him into participating fully and so consciously in the human suffering involved in the resolution of the divine self-contradiction in history. This is the ground meaning of history at the personal and collective level.

Yaweh's shame and moral defeat, in contrast to Job's superior morality and power of discrimination, become, for Jung, the motive for the Incarnation. In the Christ event the opposites of good and evil, Christ and Satan, brothers of the same Father, split totally apart. For the first time religious humanity sees the one God as it is itself, absolutely good and absolutely evil. The Christ figure, who affirms himself as wholly good, dies between absolute affirmation and denial, the divinely grounded yea and nay. In this death the Christ figure as symbol of suffering humanity becomes fully conscious of the self-contradiction in the ground of consciousness, that is, in God, just as God consciously participates for the first time in the human suffering of this contradiction.

The cost of the resolution of the divine contradiction is the death of that consciousness (everyone's) caught in individual or societal identification with one pole in the divine contradiction. The movement to the resolution of this contradiction, symbolized as resurrection in the Christian myth, is always a movement toward the recovery of the missing opposite and so toward a wider empathy as the substance and basis of a greater charity. For Jung the Christ figure's death in despair is the answer to Job. And what is the answer? Only in human suffering does God become conscious and real, and God's becoming real in this sense is the meaning of each life and of human history. Suffering the divine self-contradiction as it appears in one's individual life is, for Jung, "eschatological" in so much as it is the most significant contribution an individual can make to the resolution of the divine contradiction that necessitated creation. Jung's rather pointed, if not abrasive, formulation of these ground movements of the psyche takes this explicit form:

There is no evidence that Christ ever wondered about himself, or that he ever confronted himself. To this rule there is only one significant exception—the despairing cry from the Cross: "My God, my God, why hast thou forsaken me?" Here his human nature attains divinity; at that moment God experiences what it means to be a mortal man and drinks to the dregs what he made his faithful servant Job suffer. Here is given the answer to Job, and, clearly, this supreme moment is as divine as it is human, as "eschatological" as it is "psychological."[49]

The implications of this understanding of the answer to Job are many. One is that authentic human suffering is God's suffering which redeems both God and the human involved in it as two sides of one organic process. The answer throws considerable light on the psychic foundations of the Christian theme of death and resurrection too often taken as literal miracle or magic when confined to one amazing historical event.

Jung's understanding of the answer to Job implies that the universal truth of death and resurrection describes the process at work in the healing of the divine split which created human consciousness as the sole resource in which it could be perceived and resolved. In this visioning, death becomes that entry into the unconscious, the mother of all, as prelude to a risen consciousness whose extended empathy can embrace the divine opposites between which a former and lesser consciousness expired. As this process repeats in individual and societal life, a consciousness might well evolve, indeed, for Jung, would be forced to evolve by the dynamic itself, in which ever more aspects of the divine antinomy would be united in human historical consciousness.

Jung's psychological eschatology would imply that this resolution would somehow symbolically implicate the embrace of Christ and Satan as conflicting sides of the one ultimate reality. In this sense Jung's psychology is profoundly teleological and eschatological; it moves to the resolution of the divine self-contradiction in a human consciousness that brings into synthesis what divinity alone could not synthesize.

For this very reason Jung's psychology is the ultimate negation of apocalyptic consciousness, and indicts such consciousness of a willful refusal of the pain attached to working such a synthesis in favor of a unilateral triumph of an all-good God and the preferred community whose shadow is in the end destroyed.[50] Such a God and the humanity clustered about it would not only be impoverished by the loss of the damned, but would be, for Jung, a threat to the historical process itself. Modernity is

---

49. "Answer to Job," *Psychology and Religion,* CW 11, par. 647.
50. Ibid., par. 728.

well aware that in the current conflict between religious and/or political absolutes, apocalyptic consciousness and the one-sided certitudes it generates could prematurely terminate the human endeavor before it works its historical task of bringing the divine shadow to redemption in itself.

For these reasons Jung's eschatology is incompatible with those mainstream Christian eschatologies imagining a final split of the good and the damned. Rather Jung's eschatology would understand the Christian depiction of the absolute split between good and evil as a valuable differentiation of opposites grounded in divinity itself, which human discrimination must first differentiate and then unite in history. History thus moves to a consciousness that would work a union of absolute good and evil rather than eternalize their opposition.

This view of the meaning of history as resolving the divine self-contradiction can respect Christian imagery of absolute good and evil even as it surpasses it by insisting on the ultimate reunification of the split. Jung can and does appreciate the contribution Christianity has made in bringing the split into high definition. But he surpasses a Christian perspective and its related spirituality with his implication that modern spirituality and psychology must work a synthesis of these opposites and of all absolute opposites that find their origin in the ground of human consciousness and seek their resolution in it. The search for such a myth is the search at the heart of much of contemporary new age or third age mythology. A condition of whatever success such a search may enjoy is that it be done in full historical and critical consciousness of its predecessors and of the questionable outcome of such previous historical appearances.

At the end of the twelfth century, Joachim di Fiore, to whom Jung qualifiedly compares himself,[51] was sure that the third age, that of the Spirit working the unity of all opposites, was to occur in the immediate future. The Franciscan movement of the thirteenth century may have been another expression of this impulse but in its radical form was not without its own totalitarian shadow. Nor was the Third Reich in twentieth-century Germany any less intransigent than the Biblical apocalypticism of the Book of Revelation, whose hatred of any contradiction or impurity Jung likens to "severe psychosis."[52] The point to be made here is that a noncritical, too easy or premature effort to force the unities to which the symbol of the

---

51. *C.G. Jung Letters*, vol. 2, ed. G. Adler, A. Jaffe (Princeton: Princeton University Press, 1975), letter to Fr. Victor White, November 24, 1953, p. 138.
52. "Answer to Job, *Psychology and Religion,* CW 11, par. 731.

third age or age of the Spirit points can produce a greater inhumanity than the ills that precede and provoke such compelling hope in it.

What safeguards might Jung's mature psychology proffer to avoid the disasters that have plagued previous ages in their efforts to unite the opposites of the divine and human, and to unite in the human the opposites of the divine, the synthesis that so eluded Jung's father? Jung's psychology would answer along the following lines. We now realize that conscious dialogue with the unconscious in whatever form, but especially in the form of the dream, is functionally a dialogue with divinity. This realization could restore a safer religiosity to contemporary believer and nonbeliever alike, for the dialogue, at least in the nonpsychotic, would be with the Self and so with its anti-inflationary, balancing influence on consciousness. An honest and prolonged dialogue with the Self thus becomes the ultimate counter to the fanaticism and unconsciousness that hope in the new age can so easily engender.

Difficult though it be in the face of contemporary institutional religious and secular forces, both of which hold such dialogue in contempt, we must cultivate the sense that we are in immediate contact with the wisdom that tradition understands to be accessed only in "revelation" granted to exceptional individuals from whose power various religions, often supporting political establishments, derive their "historical" origins. We must become more at home with the idea of private revelation, whose major medium is the dream. The purpose of this is progressively to ground us in our essential being and mythology as the personal foundation from which to deal with the potentially pathologizing collective mythologies into which we may be born.

This perspective would be fully aware that the deepest meaning of suffering in one's own life is the resolution of that side of the divine self-contradiction that can only find resolution there. This revamped cosmology also would affirm that the Self, which first establishes and then seeks the resolution of whatever form of suffering becomes the ground theme of an individual life, is the power of God engaging us in a process in which God is healed in the healing of human suffering.

Should this understanding of humanity's access to divine energies prevail, it would obviate in principle the meaningless suffering inflicted on Jung's father by his religion. At the heart of his father's suffering was his removal from the divine energy of the psyche through its projection beyond the psyche, uprooting him from his groundedness in God as a sustaining inner power. The gospel or "good news" thus read becomes a blueprint for depression.

Jung's critique of Biblical imagery insisting on a deity beyond the psyche forces contemporary spirituality to ask if there is the possibility of a nonpathologizing Biblical spirituality. If there is such a possibility in the canon of Christian wisdom, it would rest in the recovery of that slender gnostic content which evaded exclusion from the canon and continues to point to the reality of humanity's natural divinity and its sustaining, balancing vitalities. This strategy could become crucial in allaying the betrayal of maturation to Gods (and even Goddesses) foreign to the humanity which creates them as alien externalizations of humanity's most precious energies.

Such dawning religious consciousness would be a major force in making a thing of the past the spiritual and human atrocity that was worked on Jung's father and on those who continue to embrace his kind of faith.

2

Jung and the White, Buber Exchanges: Exercises in Futility

The previous chapter showed that Jung's early experience of religion in his own life and in that of his father was very negative. Yet his interest in religion continued throughout his lifetime, in large part because he could not deny the religious import of so many of the expressions of the psyche with which he was confronted as a psychiatrist.

From such unlikely origins his psychology was eventually to identify in the psyche "an authentic religious function."[53] Effectively this was the basis of Jung's understanding of humanity as the "image of God," in so much as this function worked to make whole those lives open to it. Jung's psychology has thus attracted the widespread attention of religionists because of its claim to have identified the origins of religious experience in the human psyche itself.[54] This can be viewed as favorable to religion and to its study, for it supports the notion that human consciousness is in and of itself incorrigibly religious. Others have attacked Jung's claim as undermining religion itself. This response is particularly evident with those who identify true religion with its concretization in one or other preferred revelation, taken as a definitive historical incursion into human affairs by a wholly transcendent God.

The defensive response to Jung is dramatically evidenced in his exchanges with Martin Buber, the Jewish religious thinker, and with Victor White, O.P., a Dominican and Thomist, and so a representative of the then presiding Roman Catholic theological tradition. These dialogues exemplify the threat Jung's psychology represented to transcendentalist theologies. Yet, paradoxically, a sustained examination of the reasons for the failed dialogues with Buber and White contributes to an understanding of the religious and metaphysical import of Jung's psychology.

Such an inquiry suggests that the latent foundational incompatibilities of

---

53. "Psychology and Religion," ibid., par. 3.
54. See "Introduction to the Religious and Psychological Problems of Alchemy," *Psychology and Alchemy*, CW, 12, par. 9.

Jung's psychology with the transcendentalism, supernatural dualism and sophisticated fundamentalism of Buber and White precluded a successful outcome of the dialogues in principle and from the outset. At the same time the dialogues themselves served to make the foundational incompatibilities between the conversants blatantly apparent.

Buber initiated the discussion with Jung in an article entitled "Religion and Modern Thinking,"[55] which appeared in the German journal *Merkur* in February, 1952. In it Buber points back to "a very early writing"[56] in which Jung first expressed his gnostic leanings. He was referring to a piece of poetry Jung had written in 1916, namely *Septem Sermones ad Mortuos* (Seven Sermons to the Dead).[57] In his later reply to Buber, Jung was to describe this poetry as "a sin of my youth."[58]

This was hardly a very candid statement on Jung's part if by it he meant to imply that after his youth he moved away from a gnostic sensitivity. To anyone who reads primary Jung, it is simply undeniable that Jung's appreciation of gnostic religiosity, understood as an unmediated experience of the unconscious and its religion-making powers, remained firmly in place throughout his mature writings. For Buber such unmediated intercourse between divine and human was greatly exaggerated. It served only to corrode modernity's sense of the true transcendent God. It is not surprising then that in his article Buber linked Jung with Sartre and Heidegger as contributing to the modern "eclipse of God."[59]

Buber's case against Jung in his opening attack thus centers on the charge that Jung's psychology was a sophisticated form of that reductionism known as psychologism, and was imbued with a profound gnostic element which too intimately related the divine and the human. Such gnosis allegedly vested the human with an illegitimate knowledge of the religious mystery, illegitimate because beyond the competence of the human. Buber's was a well-stated variant of a charge made in more than one form against Jung's psychology. Indeed it was on one occasion cited by Jung himself when he admitted the difficulties involved with the contemporary

---

55. The Jung-Buber correspondence is documented in "Religion and Psychology: A Reply to Martin Buber," *The Symbolic Life*, CW 18, par. 1501, note 1.
56. Martin Buber, "Religion and Modern Thinking," *Eclipse of God* (New York: Harper and Row, 1952), p. 85.
57. *Memories, Dreams, Reflections*, Appendix 5, pp. 378ff.
58. "A Reply to Martin Buber," *The Symbolic Life*, CW 18, par. 1501.
59. "Religion and Modern Thinking," *Eclipse of God,* pp. 63f.

religious mind in his efforts to reroot humanity in its native sense of divinity. Jung is obviously referring to charges such as Buber's when he writes that anyone engaged in such a task is inevitably accused of " 'psychologism' or suspected of morbid 'mysticism.' "[60]

Of course, Buber's charge of gnosticism and reductionism implies that Buber himself clearly knew where the legitimate boundaries of human knowledge of the divine lay and how the divine and human interrelate in their experience of each other. Indeed his description of what divinity is and how it relates to humanity is frankly laid out in this article. Buber variously describes this divine being as "that absolute Other, the absolute over against me,"[61] and "One who is experienced or believed in as being absolutely over against one."[62] In his later reply to Jung's response, Buber further describes this absolute Other as a "super-psychic Being"[63] and "an extra-psychical Being."[64] His central concern is that such a Being exists independently of the psyche or of what he calls "the human subject."[65] His fear is that Jung's psychology denies such transcendent independence of deity. Buber's obvious uneasiness with radical human subjectivity forces his conclusion, in fact a correct one properly understood, that Jung's psychology amounts to a religion of "pure psychic immanence."[66]

In a second distinct line of argument, both in his original charge and in his rejoinder, Buber argues that Jung's concept of the Self as made up of the unity of opposites, including good and evil, is the basis for a form of moral libertinism. Here he cites Jung's usage of Carpocrates, identified as a gnostic by no less an authority than Iranaeus himself.[67] Jung does indeed cite Carpocrates (three times) in his *Collected Works*[68] to point to the necessity of assimilating the shadow in the process of individuation.[69]

For Jung, becoming conscious of the shadow would entail the painful

---

60. "Psychological Commentary on The Tibetan Book of the Great Liberation," *Psychology and Religion,* CW 11, par. 771.
61. *Eclipse of God,* p. 68.
62. Ibid., p. 78.
63. Ibid., p. 134.
64. Ibid., p. 135.
65. Ibid., p. 133.
66. Ibid., p. 84.
67. Ibid., p. 137.
68. See "Woman in Europe," *Civilization in Transition,* CW 10, par. 271; "Psychology and Religion," *Psychology and Religion,* CW 11, par. 133; *Mysterium Coniunctionis,* CW 14, par. 284.
69. "Psychology and Religion," *Psychology and Religion,* CW 11, par. 133.

and steadfast staring at the potential for evil in one's personal being. Such confrontation is the first step in the transformation of the shadow through its appropriation into an expanded and safer consciousness less susceptible to projecting personal or collective evil onto others. In the context of Jung's psychology, such rigorous honesty is a far cry from moral irresponsibility. On the contrary, the moral demand to confront one's shadow grounds a harrowing, life-long self-examination under the scrutiny of the Self, whose critique of one's conscious position is made most tellingly through dreams. Such a process demands a far more prolonged and wider examination of conscience and penitential sensitivity than collective religion can provide. Jung is explicit in his statement that such morally rigorous, often humiliating, shadow work is the work of a lifetime.[70]

Jung replied to Buber in the May issue of the same journal in which Buber had launched his attack. His reply took three major thrusts. First he fell back on a position he frequently took in other discussions with theologians, namely, that he was first and foremost an empiricist and not a metaphysician.[71] In evaluating Jung's first line of response one must try to make some sense of what he meant by these terms.

Let us first examine his claim to be an empiricist. Jung stretched the term "empiricism" to include more than those archetypal statements made by the mythologies and religions of the world. This material is usually accepted as empirical if for no more compelling reason than that it can be catalogued—and usually forgotten—in dictionaries of folklore or religion. But Jung extends the meaning to include psychological material drawn from dreams, hallucinations and fantasies. Frequently this material bears an amazing and empirical—that is, demonstrable—likeness to themes in religion and folklore. Thus the data base, if one can use so crude a term, of Jung's empiricism would include both the world religions and such current expressions of the psyche as the nightly dream or waking hallucination. This data base came to support Jung's mature conviction that both personal dream and collective revelation are expressions of the same generative source, the collective unconscious. If one can thus extend the meaning of the word, Jung was indeed an empiricist and his approach, both theoretically and therapeutically, was, indeed, empirical.

His discussion of metaphysics is more complex. His use of the term

---

70. *Mysterium Coniunctionis*, CW 14, par. 759. Jung writes typically, "Always we shall have to begin again from the beginning."
71. "Reply to Martin Buber," *The Symbolic Life*, CW 18, par. 1502.

yields at least three senses throughout his work. Occasionally he will argue that metaphysics, as philosophy, is simply a systematized expression of the dominant complex in the philosopher's psyche. Depicting metaphysics as an unconscious expression of the unconscious would explain the apparent permanence of the practice in the face of its consistent failure to achieve any substantial agreement among its practitioners. The subtle irony of this position is evident when Jung endorses Nietzsche's suggestion that metaphysics for the modern should become the "ancilla psychologiae,"[72] the handmaiden of psychology. By such remarks Jung means that, just as certain mediaeval theologians would understand philosophy as the handmaiden of theology—which alone, informed with the gift of supernatural and infused faith, could explain philosophy's full meaning to it—so modern depth psychology could explain to today's metaphysician or theologian what complex compelled his or her metaphysics or theological faith.[73]

In the second sense he gives the term, Jung will occasionally refer to his own metaphysical aspirations and to himself as a "philosopher *manqué,*"[74] in thinly disguised recognition, never fully acknowledged, of the philosophical implications of his psychology. In so much as metaphysics can be understood as concerned with what is and how it is known, his psychology does indeed include a latent metaphysic and Jung could have been more candid in admitting it. Indeed it was Buber's clear perception of the metaphysical implications of Jung's psychology which so threatened him and drove him to his initial attack.

But in its third and most frequently used sense, which grounds his denials of dabbling in metaphysics in his discussions with theologians, Jung means a body of knowledge for which there is neither compelling internal (subjective) evidence nor external (objective) evidence, that is, a body of knowledge for which there is no evidence at all. In no small measure he derived this meaning from his youthful observations, as we have seen, that his clerical father and uncles, when discussing matters theological and dogmatic, had absolutely no experiential sense of what they were talking about.[75] In this sense metaphysics can be related to what he later called the

---

72. "On the Nature of the Psyche," *The Structure and Dynamics of the Psyche,* CW 8, par. 344.
73. Ibid., par. 346. See also, "Basic Postulates of Analytical Psychology," ibid., par. 659.
74. *C. G. Jung Letters,* vol. 1, letter to F. Seifert, July 31, 1935, p. 194.
75. *Memories, Dreams, Reflections,* pp. 73f.

"sacrosanct unintelligibility"[76] of religious dogma, the sacred meaning-lessness of statements that once bore the energies of the unconscious but now are dead. Metaphysics thus understood can best be described as a blind faith divested of any experiential basis in the human. Thus the term applies to those, among whom he includes Buber, "who for one reason or another think they know about unknowable things in the Beyond." [77]

In a later reference to the Buber interchange, Jung likens the metaphysical capacity to "an organ" enabling the believer thus vested to "tune in the Transcendent."[78] But he denies, and here he appeals to Kant, that such knowledge can ever be a public possession. Rather, wherever operative, such metaphysical faith is grounded in archetypal experience, indeed possession, of which the believer usually remains unconscious. For Jung such archetypal experience bears both the imaginal content of the so-called metaphysical faith and the energies that compel belief in it, though the origin of both usually remains unknown to the "believing" individual. It is in this sense that Jung claims he is possessed of no such organ and so is not a metaphysician, while implying that Buber's faith and sense of God are based on an archetypal possession of which Buber remained unaware.

Jung's second line of response to Buber rests on foundational elements of his own psychology of religion. It identifies in the power of the archetypes, here termed "immanent-transcendent,"[79] and in their imagery projected beyond the psyche, those energies which create the Gods and Goddesses and their disparate revelations. Thus dialogue with the divine Thou, which Buber understands as the absolute Other, becomes for Jung dialogue with the unconscious and its archetypal powers as the source of "everything one could wish for . . . in the psychic Thou."[80] It is on this foundational issue of the location, so to speak, of the Other that the views of the two are most incompatible. Jung locates the Other in those dimensions of the psyche which infinitely transcend the ego but with which the ego remains organically continuous in the life of the psyche. Buber locates the Other in a heaven beyond the psyche.

The final line of Jung's response, again a wider theme in his work, centered on the difficulty of distinguishing which of the divine contenders

---

76. See above, note 10.
77. "Reply to Martin Buber," *The Symbolic Life,* CW 18, par. 1503.
78. *C. G. Jung Letters*, vol. 2, letter to Bernhard Lang, June 1957, p. 375.
79. "Reply to Martin Buber," *The Symbolic Life,* CW 18, par. 1505.
80. Ibid., par. 1504.

was in fact the true Objective One whom Buber insisted existed beyond the psyche. Here Jung touches somewhat sardonically on a problem which is obvious to all, but still defiant of any significant religious or theological solution. He writes:

> Consequently I do not permit myself the least judgement as to whether and to what extent it has pleased a metaphysical deity to reveal himself to the devout Jew as he was before the Incarnation, to the Church Fathers as the Trinity, to the Protestants as the one and only Saviour without co-redemptrix and to the present Pope as a saviour with co-redemptrix.[81]

In these passages he goes on to wonder where the deities of the Eastern religions fit into the divine squabble for exclusive ultimacy.

The impatience, even pique, evidenced in these lines is again all too apparent when Jung suggests that a trip through an asylum by any interested observer—among whom he obviously meant to include Buber—would illuminate both the origin of religious metaphysical ideas and the conviction with which they are held:

> It should not be overlooked that what I am concerned with are psychic phenomena which can be proved empirically to be the bases of metaphysical concepts, and that when, for example, I speak of "God" I am unable to refer to anything beyond these demonstrable psychic models which, we have to admit, have shown themselves to be devastatingly real. To anyone who finds their reality incredible I would recommend a reflective tour through a lunatic asylum.[82]

Given the irritable tone of Jung's reply, compared to Buber's evenness of writing and self-assurance, there can be little doubt who won the debate in terms of literary style and suavity. Nor does the exchange leave much doubt that Jung, on his part, was emotionally involved in the issues at stake. Buber had touched a tender spot in one who denied a metaphysical implication in such conceptions as the archetypes and the nature of their influence on consciousness as the basis of humanity's religious instinct. Buber had rightly perceived the threat to the credibility of a transcendent and self-sufficient one and only God posed by Jung's psychology, and Jung might have been more open in simply affirming that indeed such implications were there.

---

81. Ibid., par. 1507.
82. Ibid., par. 1506.

However, the interchange did bring out quite clearly what, in fact, Buber's conditions were for the divinity to whom one related as an I to a Thou. Such a divinity was exposed as the all-too-familiar, wholly transcendent and monotheistic deity who would somehow be eclipsed if He were to be understood as grounded in the psyche. The exchange leaves it very clear that the divine Thou to whom Buber relates the human I is in no significant sense a function of the depth of human subjectivity in the orders of being, knowing or morality. In the light of the conversation with Jung, Buber's suggestions of intimacy between the divine Thou and the human I are revealed as little more than religious poetry whose metaphysical implications Buber could neither face nor accept.

An examination of Jung's relationship with Victor White reveals a final parting of the ways for many of the same philosophical and theological reasons. Jung was to write in a later letter that his relation with Buber was always polite. Yet the truth was that they had never enjoyed a close personal friendship. This was not the case with Victor White.

Jung was a close friend of White's for some sixteen years, from their initial correspondence in 1945 until White's death at the age of fifty-eight in 1960. Their relationship began when White, then professor of dogmatic theology at Blackfriars, in Oxford, England, sent Jung a series of articles that he had written and published on Jung's psychology and its theological implications.[83] From his early letters to White, Jung clearly felt that finally he had found a theologian who understood his psychology and the "enormous implications" of seriously relating depth psychology to theology in the modern epoch.[84]

Over the course of the years White frequently visited Jung in Zürich and at his retreat in Bollingen, where only the truly favored were invited. It is obvious from the correspondence that Jung was analyzing White's dreams and working with him in other processes of discernment concerning the direction White's life should take.[85] It also seems that White was in fact conducting what today would be understood as an analytic practice.[86]

---

83. *C. G. Jung Letters,* vol. 1, p. 381, Sept. 26, 1945.
84. Ibid., p. 383, letter of October 5, 1945.
85. See, for instance, ibid, p. 448, note 1, and p. 490, note 2; see also the letter of April 10, 1954, pp. 169-170.
86. See ibid., vol. 2, p. 171, letter of April 10, 1954. Jung writes, "Being an analyst, you know how little you can say, and sometimes it is quite enough when only the analyst knows."

The first point of serious contention surfaced as early as 1949 over White's understanding of evil as a "privatio boni," a traditional theological conception of evil as having no substance in itself but being rather an absence of good.[87] For Jung the point was both academic and clinical. In a foreword to a book written by White, Jung describes a case in which "a scholarly man" was using the denial of the reality of evil simply to ease his conscience in the face of his "morally reprehensible practices."[88] This became a living and major issue between them, because it forced Jung to make explicit his own considered position, namely, that evil had its own reality and could no more be defined as the absence of good than cold could be defined as the absence of heat, or dark the absence of light.

The issue for Jung moved directly to the question of how seriously White and the Christian mind could take the reality of evil not only as it existed in creation but, if creation reflected its creator, in that creator too. The question soon extended from the creator and creation to Christology and to the total split between the Christ figure embodying absolute good and Satan embodying absolute evil.[89]

The debate thus helped to define Jung's emerging psychological perspective as well as its cosmological and metaphysical implications. In the discussion with White, Jung came more clearly to understand the split between absolute good and evil as reflective of a contradiction in the divine ground itself. Jung came to imagine this conflicted ground giving rise both to creation, in which good and evil are undeniably present, and to the Christian myth, where the absolute contradiction between Christ as absolute good and his shadow brother Satan as absolute evil can no longer be evaded. In so far as the Christian myth made the contradiction obvious, it was, for Jung, a significant religious differentiation and substantial contribution to the evolution of humanity's religious consciousness. But by the same psychological logic, the Christian myth could not be ultimate because it lacked the symbol to unite the absolute divinely grounded contradiction it so dramatically revealed. As such it remained a penultimate stage in humanity's religious development now pleading for its own supercession.

Through the prolonged exercise of these wider issues, the discussions with White contributed to Jung's formulations of the all-encompassing dy-

---

87. Ibid., vol. 1, p. 540, letter of December 31, 1949.
88. "Foreword to White's 'God and the Unconscious,' " *Psychology and Religion*, CW 11, par. 457.
89. *C. G. Jung Letters*, vol. 2, November 24, 1953, pp. 133-138.

namic of the psyche. In his later work, the psyche's movement to maturation is one of conscious differentiation and then unification of conflictual absolute opposites—good and evil in the discussion with White—which are ultimately grounded in the generative source or creator of consciousness itself. Putting the implications of Jung's psychology into a religious idiom, this meant that the ground of consciousness and being, God as creator, is necessitated to create in order to resolve in human consciousness a contradiction that defied resolution within the divine life itself.

In the mature Jung, this resolution became the meaning of both individual life and the life of humanity as a whole. To borrow from the twelfth-century mind of Joachim di Fiore, this meant that all opposites latent in God as creator were to be differentiated in the age of the Son in history and united in the future age of the Spirit. This reunification would of course include the two major unresolved opposites differentiated so well in the figures of Christ and Satan in the Christian myth.

As Jung's position on these matters took shape, White saw clearly the implied contemporary inadequacy of the image of Christ as an image of the Self, because of its one-sided spiritual nature, its lack of shadow.[90] When White pointed this out to Jung, the substance of Jung's reply was that the same Spirit that had constellated the one-sided perfection of the Christ figure over against the Satanic was now moving to unite the two. But the mode of such union and the symbol needed to effect it was beyond the power of reason to achieve.[91]

The inefficacy of reason to produce a new mythology out of its own meager resources is the basis of Jung's again frequently repeated motto, *tertium non datur*. The phrase means for him that the "third," the union of conflicting but valid opposites, was not logically foreseeable. The symbol or myth that could unite the absolute opposites differentiated so well in the Christian myth would, no doubt, abrogate the myth itself. However, in Jung's estimate, such a symbol to be authentic would surface legitimately only through faithfully suffering the now pathological one-sidedness of Christianity to a psychic death from which would rise the mythic consciousness capable of uniting Christ and Satan. In this process neither the puny power of reason nor a premature jettisoning of the presiding myth would be of any significant or longlasting use.[92]

---

90. Ibid., p. 134, note 1, and p. 163, note 1.
91. See ibid., pp. 163f, the key letter of April 10, 1954.
92. Ibid. This is the thrust of the letter of November 24, 1953, pp. 133-138.

This position, central to Jung's mature psychology, is what contemporary Jungian scholars identify as his shift from a Trinitarian to a quaternitarian paradigm.[93] This implicates a new cosmology, metaphysics and religiosity which belie Jung's claim that his psychology is free of such enterprise. Driven to this countermyth and metaphysic by what he considered the psychologically demonstrable one-sidedness of the Christian myth, which is unable to deal with the instinctual, the demonic or the feminine in either its Trinity or messiah,[94] Jung, helped by his dialogue with White, came to the position that God as creator must include at least potentially all that is manifest in creation. This would have to extend, therefore, to the demonic, to the material, bodily world and to the feminine. This paradigm implies that a Divine source, in which all opposites are latent but undifferentiated, creates human consciousness as that sole power which first perceives and then resolves the Divine contradictions in a process best described as the mutual redemption of consciousness and its Divine matrix.

Needless to say, this is a process in which the ground of consciousness, and consciousness itself, are involved by their very nature. The fourth, which necessarily completes and replaces the idea of a self-sufficient and shadowless Trinity, is humanity itself. In the context of Jung's superseding myth and its intricate dialectic, human consciousness becomes the only container in which the divine self-contradiction, now imagined as divinity's necessitating compulsion in the creation of human consciousness, is consciously perceived and hopefully resolved with the help and at the insistence of the conflicted source itself.

All these issues are explicit in the White-Jung correspondence. When White saw them exposed methodically yet poetically in Jung's "Answer to Job," he was at first enthused.[95] However, his enthusiasm turned to rejection and led him to question Jung's motives and the prudence of printing the work at that time.[96]

In spite of their later heated exchanges, in the last few years there were expressions of good will. When White died in 1960 Jung was almost

---

93. See Murray Stein, *Jung's Treatment of Christianity* (Wilmette, IL: Chiron Publications, 1985), pp. 111ff. The basis for it is Jung's essay, "A Psychological Approach to the Dogma of the Trinity," *Psychology and Religion,* CW 11.
94. See my *The Illness That We Are: A Jungian Critique of Christianity* (Toronto: Inner City Books, 1984), chapter 5, "Theopathology and Christopathology."
95. See *C. G. Jung Letters,* vol 2, p. 238, note 1, where reference is made to a favorable review of "Answer to Job" by White in *Spring 1952* (no. 6).
96. Ibid., p. 238, note 1.

eighty-five and a final reconciliatory meeting in England which Jung had hoped for proved impossible because of his health. In the end Jung felt that White's theological background made it impossible for him to grasp the more intimate paradigm of the divine-human relation that Jung sought so consistently to articulate in his psychology. In some of the sadder, more poignant lines in his letters, Jung writes to a mutual acquaintance of the meaning he saw in White's untimely death:

> I have now seen quite a number of people die in the time of a great transition, reaching as it were the end of their pilgrimage in sight of the Gates, where the way bifurcates to the land of Hereafter and to the future of mankind and its spiritual adventure.[97]

In these words Jung implies as clearly as was appropriate that the meaning of White's death was not unrelated to White's lengthy struggle with the clash between Jung's psychology and his own theology. White's theology was predicated on a supernatural, self-sufficient and perfect deity in no need of the world of created nature nor in organic continuity with it and with human consciousness. It is not surprising, then, that White could not make the transition to the sense of a more intimate relation of divinity to humanity which Jung, in this letter, contends is the face of the human religious future. To make such a transition would have cost White his faith. His failure to make it may have cost him his life.

In the end, Jung's discussions with Buber and White unite the latter two across the differences of their traditions. Their conversations with Jung revealed that the God in whom they commonly believed was a wholly other and transcendent, supernatural, self-sufficient being. Such a being is not organically linked with human consciousness as the sole agency needed by Divinity in the process of its becoming conscious. For neither Buber nor White could the depth meaning of human history be understood as the process of God's becoming conscious through humanity's suffering the divine self-contradiction. From Jung's perspective the discussions reveal that his psychology could not tolerate such a distant God uninvolved in the heart of human suffering. Nor could it endorse the supernatural dualism and disguised fundamentalism so thinly concealed by such conceptions of deity.[98]

---

97. Ibid., letter to the Mother Prioress of a contemplative order, October 19, 1960, p. 604.
98. For an elaboration of the conception of fundamentalism used here, see my ar-

Jung remains indebted to both Buber and White for making the incompatibility of his psychology with their theologies so clear, first to himself and then to those who follow and continue to be fascinated by the religious implications and alternatives of his understanding of the psyche.

The following chapters turn to the task of making explicit the implied alternative metaphysic and religiosity endemic to Jung's understanding of the psyche. By identifying the religious impulse in the psyche itself, he makes of religious experience a universal necessity grounded in human interiority in such a way that religion's expressions cannot be denied, though none may claim finality for itself. Thus his psychology appreciates religious experience while making it safer for humanity.

This metaphysic implies a spirituality which would understand the spirits to originate in the archetypal energies of the unconscious forever seeking fuller incarnation in human consciousness, and a morality which demands of humanity the recognition of its role in the always dangerous birthing of deity in history. This would necessarily involve an intensified appreciation of the psychologically subjective. Serious consideration of such a metaphysic is unfortunately absent or muted in past or current orthodox spiritualities.

To the Jungian alternative we now turn.

---

ticle, "The Challenge of Jung's Psychology for the Study of Religion," in *Studies in Religion*, vol. 18, no. 3 (1989), esp. p. 311: "In the field of religion this normative aspect of Jung's hermeneutic could lead to a new understanding of fundamentalism and of fundamentalist theology. Fundamentalism would be seen as that form of unconsciousness which is induced in the mind of the believer grasped and imprisoned by the archetypal power of the cherished myth. That theology could then be identified as fundamentalist in which the believing mind reflecting on its myth in the doing of theology remained unaware of the origin in the unconscious of both the myth itself and of the faith in the myth which prompts theological reflection upon it."

3

Interiority, Universality and Relativity: Ground Values of the Psyche

At the core of Jung's psychology is the process he calls individuation. It is a process in which the ego, the center of individual consciousness, is progressively pervaded by the truth and power of the Self.

As Jung describes it, the process of individuation, to the extent that it is realized in any life, carries with it both a sense of personal wholeness, understood as the unification of the many and often conflicting components of one's personal being, and a more inclusive empathy for all that is beyond oneself. Thus understood, individuation works apparently opposite effects. It works to achieve the highest degree of individual integration and affirmation while relating the individual ever more sympathetically to the totality. This latter aspect distinguishes Jung's understanding of individuation from individualism and falsifies charges that his psychology promotes an irresponsible individuality.

What peculiar dynamics, then, would Jung attribute to the process of individuation to account for its capacity to achieve the apparently opposite effects of a heightened sense of the individual's most abiding truth *and* an extended relatedness? The process is for Jung both intensely personal and yet always relational because it reconnects the individual to his or her native groundedness in the source or matrix of the totality.[99] Because this matrix is the basis of each individual psyche, the process takes place within the psyche whose boundaries Jung admittedly extends to infinity. This extension is implicit in Jung's understanding of the full inventory of the psyche but is made explicit when, for instance, he describes the unconscious as "of indefinite extent with no assignable limits."[100]

This wholly intrapsychic nature of individuation is the ultimate meaning

---

99. See "Psychological Commentary on 'The Tibetan Book of the Great Liberation,' " *Psychology and Religion,* CW 11, par. 782. Here Jung uses "matrix mind" as a synonym for "universal mind." (par. 760) Both phrases suggest the conscious mind is continuous with the source of mind which is also the source of its conscious archetypal expressions.
100. "Transformation Symbolism in the Mass," ibid., par. 390.

of the term "containment" for Jung. The term means that the individual's reunification with the source of personal integration and other-relatedness—the reality religionists, theologians and devotees call God—occurs entirely within the psyche of the individual. In this sense the recovery or discovery of the Self is a process that necessarily entails an enhanced universal relatedness because it engages personal consciousness with the source of all that is. Examined in terms of its impact on the individual, experiential engagement with this source, insists Jung, submits the many complexes which make up any personality, including the ego, to the service of the emerging Self. Thus patterns of individual integration and extended relatedness are invariably present as the hallmarks of individuation.

Since this process has so many sides, its characteristic movements need always to be given greater clarity in the interests of allowing modernity to understand and appreciate the full scope of Jung's understanding of human maturation. Thus this chapter argues that the elaboration of the process of individuation reveals it to be one of a radical interiority, relating the individual to the universal source of those energies within the psyche. These energies manifest in an inexhaustible and so necessarily relative manner in the archetypal experience and expression of humanity.

Moreover, it argues that the consciousness toward which the process moves carries with it an experience which must be called religious. The religious experience that attaches to processes of individuation frees the experience from any kind of ecclesial monopoly. To recognize the experience as wholly natural is not to deny that religious traditions may foster it, since it is to such experiences that they owe their origin and whatever life-enhancing potential they may continue to possess.

Indeed, if Jung is right in identifying the experience of personal integration informed by a more universal relatedness with that of the experience of grace, it would be difficult to deny the endemically religious nature of individuation. That he does identify the experience of God or grace with that of the Self is made explicit when he writes of the experience of the Self as something which can no more be forced than that of grace.

> The method cannot, however, produce the actual process of unconscious compensation; for that we depend upon the unconscious psyche or the "grace of God"—names make no difference.[101]

---

101. "Psychological Commentary on The Tibetan Book of the Great Liberation," ibid., par. 779.

That this statement is not peripheral to the general thrust of Jung's psychology is evident when he writes, again typically:

> The self then functions as a union of opposites and thus constitutes the most immediate experience of the Divine which it is psychologically possible to imagine.[102]

The radical nature of Jung's conception of containment is also made explicit in the light of the epistemology which Jung understands to be operative in the psyche itself, namely that humanity is not capable of knowing anything beyond the psyche or unmediated by the psyche. "Not only does the psyche exist, it is existence itself."[103] Quite clearly Jung is identifying humanity's experience of God with the experience of the Self. In doing so, though he may occasionally waffle on this issue, he effectively denies that a humanizing experience of the divine is accessible in any other way.

Nor can the charge of elitism be launched against Jung and his rather sophisticated understanding of the religious dimension of psychic maturation, since quite clearly he does not understand processes of individuation to be epiphenomenal or occasional to humanity's deeper experience of the fully human. On the contrary, such experience is grounded in the nature of the psyche itself and is the universal basis of humanity's religious propensity and experience.

Here Jung is consciously working with the psychological basis of the ontological argument.[104] He is fully aware that his psychology stands in a certain continuity with Anselm (1033-1109) and those sides of the mind of Augustine (354-430) which located the basis of the human experience of God in human interiority. Yet Jung departs from these giants of Christian Platonism by identifying the origins of the experience of the divine in the psyche and, more, confining the dialogue with the divine to the dialogue between the ego and its generative precedent in the interests of both truth and moral responsibility that follows from this truth.

From Jung's perspective, a dialogue with divinities transcendent to or wholly other than the psyche is thus at best infantile and at worst immoral. In this he denies the breaking of containment which plagues Christian and

---

102. "Transformation Symbolism in the Mass," ibid., par. 396.
103. "Psychology and Religion," ibid., par. 18; see also ibid., par. 16, where much the same point is made.
104. See his discussion in *Psychological Types*, CW 6, on "The Problem of Universals in Scholasticism," especially par. 61.

religious thinkers when they associate an inescapable human experience
with an originating power beyond the psyche. To Jung the sustenance of
the inner dialogue becomes the basis of a conscious religion and morality.
To avoid divinity's impelling nearness by projecting it into the sky remained for him an evasion of the living God and an option only for a
puerile spirituality.

This problem plagued Jung's life and still confronts us. What for him
was the immediate experience of God was for his theological age, and
ours, a form of psychological reductionism. His weariness at theological
insensitivity to religious experience may have begun with his father, but is
evident much later, as we have seen, when he writes of being accused of
"psychologism" or morbid "mysticism."[105]

Hence, for Jung, the possibility of a religionless humanity is not a real
one. Where such a condition is desired or proclaimed to exist in the name
of the secular or of some political program, it is but an unconscious expression of the same forces in the psyche that create religion. Such
proclamations remain unconscious of their religious aura derived from
their origin in the unconscious. As such they are as dangerous as formal
religion when they possess a community in the name of something less
readily identifiable than religion, though as numinous and irresistible in its
appeal.

This critique of faith, so much a part of Jung's psychology, enables the
modern to address consciously, possibly for the first time in the evolution
of the mind, the religion-making and deity-creating propensities of the unconscious and to evaluate them as humanity's greatest resource and gravest
threat, especially as they operate in political guise. In this respect Jung's
psychology, as profoundly introverted as it is, makes a significant political
contribution to a survival strategy precisely in its understanding of religion. It does so because it holds out to currently divided and conflicting
communities of belief, whether political or religious, the possibility of
transcending their current faiths toward a more inclusive consciousness
without betraying their legitimate instincts. In this sense the wider empathies bred by the process of individuation make of it a political act.

Thus the process of individuation bears scrutiny in its personal, but especially in its social or political dynamics. As personal experience, the dynamics of the birth of the Self are well known and are the substance of in-

---

105. See above, note 60.

dividual dream work done in the analytic hour. The Self may begin its emergence into consciousness through shadow work, the conscious assimilation of all those legitimate but denied potentials which clamor for admission into consciousness, potentials which can destroy a life too long denying them entry. Assimilation of the shadow can alter and enhance the relation to the inner feminine in the male psyche and to the inner masculine in the female psyche. Out of this marriage (well depicted by the women mystics)[106] the individual's divinity is born into consciousness. This birth is not infrequently imaged by the Self as dream-maker through the symbol of a numinous child of divine or royal origins, an experience that carries with it a profound self-possession, affirmation and relatedness.

Such a process and such an experience can never be finally solipsistic or pathologically involuted. Rather the process bears with it the potential for a social consciousness better equipped to survive the threat that humanity's own religious and political compulsions pose. All of Jung's examples of the major symbols of the Self show clearly that the psyche moves toward a state of maturity in which personal fulfillment and a sense of cosmic connectedness are but two sides of one experience. By implication, the experience is maimed by the absence of either. Jung's sense of the mercurial *anima mundi*,[107] the one soul of the world manifest in the multiple variations in which it seeks human expression, informs Jung's appreciation of his preferred major images of the Self such as the mandala, the *anthropos* and the *unus mundus*, the alchemical symbol of the individual's conscious identity with the ground of all and so with all the ground expresses.

Jung was drawn to mandala symbolism because of its implication that proximity to its divine center relates consciousness to each point on the periphery and is thus the ultimate negation of eccentricity. Drawing closer to unity with divinity, the center of the psyche, in and of itself relates the individual to the totality. This aspect of mandala symbolism also drew Jung to Bonaventure's formulation of the truth of the mandala, one with possible ancestry in the Hermetic tradition: "God is an intelligible sphere whose centre is everywhere and whose circumference is nowhere."[108]

---

106. See my essay, "Love, Celibacy and the Inner Marriage: Jung and Mechthilde of Magdeburg," in *Love, Celibacy and the Inner Marriage* (Toronto: Inner City Books, 1987), pp. 25f.
107. See *Alchemical Studies*, CW 12, par. 265: "The idea of the *anima mundi* coincides with that of the collective unconscious whose centre is the self."
108. Jung cites this phrase in various places, for instance: *Mysterium Coniuncti-*

Union with the God who is at the center of the psyche relates the individual to all that flows from such a center, but, by implication, without the same total embrace as the center itself would have. Unqualified relatedness to all points on the periphery would mean unqualified unity with the center, held exclusively by the divine. For the ego to wholly identify with the divine viewpoint would be to fall into the hands of the living God, a psychotic identification of the ego with its archetypal core. Such identification would be the ultimate inflation, the affirmation not that "I and the father are one" but that "I *am* the father." Psychologically the difference is crucial in discriminating between a wholesome relatedness to one's divinity and the insanity of the pseudo-messiah.

Since the center of the psyche is both the center of individual life and of the universe, its nature is always to transcend the approaching ego, even as it demands the ego's drawing near in a circumambulation psychologically impossible to evade without destruction of the soul through inflation on one hand or loss of interest in life on the other. One of Jung's most telling, yet typical descriptions of the power and charm of the Self leading the ego closer to its center concludes that "the unconscious man is made one with his centre, which is also the centre of the universe, and in this wise the goal of man's salvation and exaltation is reached."[109]

In a similar vein, in his treatment of the *anthropos* symbol, Jung seeks to describe a state of consciousness in which the individual comes increasingly to experience his or her individuality as coextensive with all that is, has been and can be human.[110] Jung relates this to various forms of mystical experience and expression ranging across specific religions, for instance in the Jewish mythical figure of Adam Kadmon[111] and in the Pauline figure of the Christ as second Adam gathering all to a final totality or apocatastasis.[112] Both these images arise from and seek to share the innately religious experience of the identity of the individual with the totality,

---

onis, CW 14, par. 41, in relation to alchemical imagery; *Psychological Types*, CW 6, par. 791, note 74, describing the mandala as identifiably a symbol of the self because of the numinosity attaching to it; "A Psychological Approach to the Dogma of the Trinity," *Psychology and Religion*, CW 11, par. 229, note 6, where Jung relates the phrase to the Hermetic tradition and gnostic thought.

109. "Transformation Symbolism in the Mass," ibid., par. 445.

110. See, for instance, "The Structure and Dynamics of the Self," *Aion*, CW, 9ii, par. 388.

111. See *Mysterium Coniunctionis*, CW 14, par. 591.

112. See "Christ, a Symbol of the Self," *Aion*, CW 9ii, pars. 71-73.

the unity of microcosm with macrocosm.

In modern times, the experience of the individual's unity with total humanity, either as present experience or as the necessary direction in which history moves, informs the vision of the young Marx. Such archetypal inspiration lies at the basis of his conviction that the human enterprise itself is destined to a universal consciousness of communion between individual and the species, impelling each individual to act spontaneously on behalf of humanity itself. The archetypal energy of the *anthropos* myth is blatant when Marx typically writes,

> Human emancipation will only be complete . . . when as an individual man, in his everyday life, in his work, and in his relationships, he has become a *species-being*; and when he has recognized and organized his own powers *(forces propres)* as social powers so that he no longer separates this *social* power from himself as *political* power.[113]

For Marx only the universal experience of the mystical unity of individual and species would ultimately destroy the bourgeois world "of atomistic, antagonistic individuals."[114]

Though the vision is breathtaking, the political and frequently forced implementation of this myth is currently breaking down after unknown numbers of human lives have been sacrificed to its charm. The wanton loss of human life to archetypal energies previously working in religious guise and now in political disguise bears stark witness to the power of the faith the archetype of the *anthropos* engenders. The political aspect of Jung's psychology in the light of the twentieth-century experience is of great value, then, for it leads to an identification of the archetypal basis of political conviction, which is the first step in avoiding or dissolving it toward a saving, more humane relativism. Jung's psychology thus provides some defense against such political addiction and the loss of life that any unchecked addiction will eventually demand.

However, this counter to political faith would mean the confrontation of powerful conflicting forces within the psyche in processes of prolonged and often painful introspection. Consequently Jung's cure for political possession remains, unfortunately, of dubious value in a Western culture still convinced that the enemy is somehow outside or beyond the psyche.

---

113. Karl Marx, "On the Jewish Question," in *The Marx-Engels Reader*, ed. Robert C. Tucker (New York: W.W. Norton & Co., 1972), pp. 44-45.
114. Ibid., p. 50.

This now possibly terminating externalism continues to be reinforced with theological paradigms of absolute good and evil. Such forces stand always and dangerously ready to lend supernatural support to forces of good fighting readily identifiable forces of evil.

The projection of intrapsychic contradictions into the sky, creating a transcendent good God and a bad Satan, is not confined to Western religiosity. Yet one can hardly deny that such unconsciousness, reinforced by institutional religion in the service of an unshakable collective faith in Western democratic and technocratic rationalism, was a major factor in the recent act of near genocide perpetrated in the Gulf War. Consciousness of the danger of collective archetypal possession and the more encompassing empathy Jung would attach to processes of individuation could only foster a political and social conscience repelled by the demonizing of others in order to justify their extermination.

In our final example of the interpenetration of individual and social in Jung's master images of the Self, the alchemical *unus mundus* presents the experience of the individual's unity with the totality as the goal of human and spiritual maturation reached through a psychic pilgrimage whose stages the alchemists clearly laid out.[115] Its first stage, which Jung implies never ends, begins with so radical a transformation that it is imaged as the death of the soul to an imprisoning embodiment.[116] This state does not imply contempt for the body but does acknowledge that the instinctual can become soul-destroying. The soul of an addict would be all too familiar with such entrapment by the instincts.

Indeed, the purpose of their separation, imaged by death, is to effect in the second stage a reunion of body and soul now animated with its true directing Spirit.[117] The process of the initially painful but ultimately joyous integration of body, soul and spirit (this stage is called a "caelum,"[118] implying heavenly consciousness) culminates in the individual's conscious intrapsychic unity with "the eternal Ground of all empirical being."[119] Now the adept perceives nature, self and humanity to participate in one world transparent in all its multiplicity to its common eternal ground.

---

115. Jung's treatment of this symbol culminates in *Mysterium Coniunctionis*, CW 14, par. 670.
116. Ibid., par. 671.
117. Ibid., par. 673.
118. Ibid., par. 770.
119. Ibid., par. 760.

Jung related his understanding of the process culminating in the experience of the *unus mundus* to the phenomenon of synchronicity: "If mandala symbolism is the psychological equivalent of the *unus mundus*, then synchronicity is its parapsychological equivalent."[120]

In this single sentence Jung is working something of a synthesis of the major symbols he uses to illustrate the process of individuation and its natively religious sensitivity. In doing so he implies that there is an organic unity to his understanding of individuation or human maturation, even though this understanding draws on such apparently diverse amplifications as crosscultural mandala symbolism, late medieval alchemical notions of personal transformation, and conceptions of synchronicity with affinities to the twentieth-century world of physics. Unpacking the connection would again contribute to the elaboration of the simple but many-sided reality of individuation processes.

Jung understood the synchronistic event as one easily dismissed as pure chance by a disinterested onlooker but as the occasion of a dramatic transformation of the life of the individual caught up in it.[121] For such an individual the synchronistic event carries an impact equivalent to being affronted personally by a divine or providential intrusion into one's life. Such events serve to establish a more residual synchronous consciousness which relates individual to totality much as does the consciousness implied by the alchemical symbol of the *unus mundus*.

Jung was influenced in his understanding of synchronicity through his work with Wolfgang Pauli (1900-1958), the Nobel Prize winning Swiss physicist who turned to Jung for help and was analyzed by one of Jung's associates.[122] One of Pauli's culminating imaginal expressions suggests that the individual is related to a center pulsing with a divine energy. It took the form of two spheres, one horizontal the other vertical, sharing a common center. Each sphere was a clock with a moving hand, but the movement of the vertical hand empowered the movement of the horizontal

---

120. Ibid., par. 662.
121. See "Synchronicity: an Acausal Connecting Principle," *The Structure and Dynamics of the Psyche*, CW 8. For a thorough discussion of Jung's conception of synchronicity and its religious implications see Robert Aziz, *C. G. Jung's Psychology of Religion and Synchronicity* (Albany: State University of New York Press, 1990).
122. See *The Symbolic Life*, CW 18, par. 673, note 9, where Pauli is identified as the man whose dream sequence is presented in *Psychology and Alchemy*, CW 12, section 2, "Individual Dream Symbolism in Relation to Alchemy."

hand as its base energy. Approximation with this center as the center of one's individuality in which vertical and horizontal meet would thus relate the individual to all that is in the external world through intersection with the vertical or "transcendental" power which moves it. After a long digression on historical variants of this symbol of the world clock, Jung is succinct in his summation of its core meaning: "And thus its innermost meaning would simply be the union of the soul with God."[123]

What attracted Jung to this image and to certain themes in modern physics was the implication that each individual is an expression of a common ground which gives rise to all individual centers of consciousness. Images of the union of consciousness with this generative substrate would thus constitute another powerful way of perceiving psychological maturation through the experience of the source of the totality in oneself.

The dramatic synchronistic event thus understood would work to convince one of the existence and power of this substrate in the interests of a more conscious relation to it. This is certainly implied in Jung's description of what happened between himself, an analysand and her dream of a golden scarab, which appeared as a rose chafer in the analytic hour subsequent to the event. He writes, "This experience punctured the desired hole in her rationalism and broke the ice of her intellectual resistance."[124] In this instance, as in most synchronistic events, suggests Jung, there is something of a desperate move on the part of the Self to demonstrate its reality in order to lead the individual into dialogue with it and toward what might be called a synchronous consciousness. A consciousness of this kind would live with a sense of being supported by the ground of all that is, and so would relate in greater harmony to both its personal and cosmic surroundings.

The foregoing discussion should make it obvious that what Jung is doing through these images of the Self is equating the process of human maturation with that of spiritual maturation. A further implication may be revealed in this correlation and might be called the mystical imperative. For Jung suggests that the process of individuation culminates in the experience of personal integration and universal relatedness, which certainly is religious and may be the substance of the mystic's experience of immersion or unqualified unity, fleeting or residual, with the source of the total-

---

123. Ibid., par. 124.
124. "On Synchronicity," *The Structure and Dynamics of the Psyche,* CW 8, par. 982. The same event is described in par. 843.

ity. The process operative in entering and disengaging from such unqualified unity will be elaborated later. Suffice it to say here that it would have to be an ongoing process of the ego's identity with the source of consciousness followed by a disidentification which would enable the return of ego-consciousness from its dissolution in its source.

This psychological process can equally well be described as incest with the Great Mother through entry into the womb of all consciousness and return from it, or, in Meister Eckhart's language, as the breakthrough to an unqualified identity with God and a return to the finite world. Thus Jung identifies and attributes a mystical yearning to "all better men as the 'longing for the mother,' the nostalgia for the source from which we came."[125] In spite of the abiding danger to the ego of such immersion in its source, sought also by addicts of all persuasions, this process is at once the most valuable of human spiritual resources and yet is as natural, one might say as demanded, as the physiological growth of organic life. In short, Jung revisions religious and mystical experience as a process as natural as growing hair, though of far greater necessity and importance.

As noted initially, the process Jung terms individuation is one which can be helpfully understood through its most distinguishing characteristics of interiorization, universalization and relativization. Each of these, and the values attaching to them, are implicated in the psyche's natural movement to that state in which religious and human maturation coincide. Reflection on these qualities of individuation points to the conclusion that humanity is incorrigibly religious and as such faces an ambiguous situation in which its life can be enhanced or destroyed by a religiosity it cannot escape. In this sense Jung's psychology is both the ultimate validation of humanity's religiosity and its most strident critic.

Interiorization

Interiorization refers to the point Jung makes so consistently throughout his work, namely that the origin of humanity's religious experience lies in the impact of archetypal energies on human consciousness. This impact invariably brings with it the sense of the numinous with which primordial religious experience is always clothed.[126]

---

125. *Two Essays on Analytical Psychology*, CW 7, par. 260.
126. See "Psychology and Religion," *Psychology and Religion*, CW 11, par. 6, where Jung describes the practice of religion as "a scrupulous observation of . . .

The most intense form of numinous experience attaches to the Self, which in projection addresses the individual with the force of deity. As mentioned above, Paul's conversion provides an example of this dynamic. The voice which accused him of persecution was heard from beyond and attributed to the Christ figure, when the true object of such persecution and subject of the voice was his suffering Self. Jung notes that such events are so powerful they naturally breed in their "victim" the misperception that they are "due to a cause external to the individual."[127] This was certainly the case with Paul. The various accounts of the Christ figure's validation by the voice of the Father, and the accounts of the Transfiguration events in which certain of the apostles also witnessed the bright light and appearance of the long-dead but religiously distinguished, would lend further weight to Jung's remarks.

Thus Jung would contend that what the Gods and Goddesses say and do in perceptible hallucination or projection beyond the psyche describe a drama that rages within it. To date, at least according to the Scriptures which record such events, this drama apparently cannot be recognized or addressed on the inner stage even by the individuals graced with such experiences. Thus human address by the Gods is experienced as originating with various deities, dictating to the human from beyond the human.

Jung's understanding of the psychogenesis of such revelation may contribute to the much-needed reversal of how the process is perceived. His psychology would identify these diverse revelations in their psychic origins and so render them all the more powerful because so personally intimate. At the same time his psychology would work to make such revelatory experiences safer for those not caught up in them. The awareness that competing sets of "revelations" or "Bibles" and "Holy Scriptures" originate in a source common to all humanity would obviate the need for conversion and lessen the friction which exists between different religious communities. Rather, competing revelations could be accepted in a spirit of awe and wonder at the variety of archetypal expressions which have possessed individual and societal consciousness in the name of faith.

In this attitude of wonder and awe, devotee and scholar could search for any overriding direction in the current history of the Spirit which these revelations may collectively and sequentially reveal. Jung's suggestion is

---

the *numinosum,*" and par. 8, where religion is described as the "careful observation and consideration" of these same energies.
127. Ibid., par. 6.

that they point the individual not toward the serial revelations of transcendent Gods with earthly spokesmen, but back to human interiority as their still active source. He writes of a now dawning consciousness: "Then everything of a divine or daemonic character outside us must return to the psyche, to the inside of the unknown man, whence it apparently originated."[128] Once this psychic source of deity is identified it could then be consciously addressed as operative in breeding a more universal myth, one capable of graciously surpassing those now extant and presiding myths with their dubious personal and social consequences.

It is precisely this radical interiority, which locates the origin of religious experience within the psyche, though in depths which transcend the ego and can take it into their service, that renders Jung's psychology incompatible in principle with theologies of supernaturalism or conceptions of human sinfulness understood to destroy humanity's sense of God. Usually such theologies also envision a divine approach to humanity from some position wholly beyond it. This externalism, literalism and historicism are the bases, as we have seen, of Jung's distancing himself from Buber and White, and of his indictment of his father's religiosity.

Jung was deeply concerned that such removal of the sense of God from human life would deprive the soul of its vitality and human suffering of its meaning. These consequences follow naturally from the supernatural externalization of God because deity in projection is deprived of that numinous impact which the experience of the Self never lacks. When such externalized deity is considered as morally perfect, the result is all the more insidious because, for Jung, the deity which humanity experiences immediately in its soul is one whose life is made up of those unreconciled opposites which must be reconciled in human consciousness. The reconciliation of these opposites in human consciousness is the only meaning of true human suffering and all that gives it dignity. To deny the soul its natural access to God is thus for Jung to debase it, and to deny the soul the suffering of the divine self-contradiction is to trivialize the reality of those who suffer it consciously. In the final analysis such transcendentalism deprives humanity, again strangely in the name of religion and theology, its status as image of God.

When these same themes are considered in their collective dimension, it becomes apparent that the substance of the philosophy of history and the

---

128. Ibid., par. 141.

history of religion, which coincide in Jung's understanding of the psyche as the source of both history and religion, is the notion that humanity's historical task is the redemption of the divine antinomy whose resolution necessitates consciousness and so history as such.[129] Interiorization as a note of individuation would imply that only in direct communication with the Self, prompted by the suffering specific to each life, can the individual perceive what aspect of the divine contradiction seeks reconciliation in that life and culture. Not only does the Self thus illuminate, indeed frequently intensify, the suffering in each life, it also provides, especially in dream symbols, the power to resolve the divinely based conflict which is the deepest meaning of every life.

This radical meaning of interiorization finds little or no supportive resonance in Western theologies. Though certain streams of ontologism, religious romanticism and pantheism in the Western tradition come close to Jung's sense of divinity's impress on consciousness, he felt his sense of divinity's experienced intimacy with the human was more to the fore in Eastern religious consciousness.[130] In the West such a compelling sense of divine immediacy had been driven to the periphery of religious respectability with the early Christian extirpation of the gnostic sensibility and with the positioning of mystical experience on the periphery of theological respectability. The fringe traditions of alchemy and the grail did preserve this more natural sense of a divine presence, a presence, it should be noted, always demanding further conscious incarnation through the arduous cooperation of those touched by it. But such traditions existed in tension with the ecclesial center rather than as welcome amplifications.[131]

Jung's analysis of the role of theology itself in uprooting Western consciousness from the sense of its native divinity is not culturally isolated. It has features in common with like analyses by Wilfrid Cantwell Smith[132]

---

129. This is the foundational import of Jung's "Answer to Job."

130. This is particularly the thrust of his work on the East in his psychological commentaries on "The Tibetan Book of the Great Liberation" and "The Tibetan Book of the Dead," in *Psychology and Religion,* CW 11.

131. For a more detailed discussion of this point, see my "How the West Was Lost," *The Illness That We Are* (Toronto: Inner City Books, 1984), pp. 27ff, and "Jung, Tillich and Aspects of Western Christian Development," *Jung and Christianity in Dialogue,* eds. Robert L. Moore and Daniel J. Meckel (New York: Paulist Press,1990), pp. 63ff. Separate Press from 1990.

132. See Chae Young Kim, *A Comparative Study of Psyche and Person in The Works of C.G. Jung and W.C. Smith,* Doctoral Thesis, Department of Religion, University of Ottawa, 1992.

and Paul Tillich.[133] That his analysis is not entirely idiosyncratic raises again the central question, whether Christianity is able to reroot the West in a living sense of God and still remain itself.

In the context of this question it should not be forgotten that Jung asked to be identified as a heretic on very solid grounds. His claim to heretical status would indicate that he himself thought the implications of his psychology were not compatible with foundational Christian dogma and theology. His most explicit self-indictment centers on his endorsement of alchemy, which he clearly understood as a form of self-salvation whose true gold is the recovery of the practitioner's natural divinity.[134]

In Western religious language this would mean that humanity as such is naturally human and divine and that the realization of its divinity is through a process of self-recovery which has little dependence on external or ecclesial mediation. This dimension of Jung's appropriation of the alchemical tradition asks the West if its mainstream theology can truly embrace the vision of a divinity so intimate to the depths of the humanity it has created and with whom it currently pleads for redemption into consciousness. It further asks if those religious sensitivities such as gnosticism, which tradition felt compelled to exclude in the process of its self-making, can now be reintroduced as the possibility of its healing.

In the final analysis, the overriding question that Jung's reading of the spiritual state of the modern psyche poses is whether or not Western Christian culture can become whole and remain Christian.

Universalization

This aspect of Jung's understanding of the psyche is fraught with difficulty to which Jung himself contributed. For he does want to establish some sense in which individuation, and more, its symbolic expressions, are truly universal. Indeed more than once he appeals to the *consensus gentium*, a psychological version of the Vincentian Canon which perceives

---

133. See especially "The Two Types of Philosophy of Religion," *Theology of Culture* (Oxford: Oxford University Press, 1959), pp. 10ff.
134. See *Psychology and Alchemy*, CW 12, par. 40, and par. 93, where he points to the Church recognition of alchemy as heretical and to the alchemists' possible attempts to disguise their true meaning; in par. 144, he identifies the alchemical heresy as the alchemists' production of the "Son," i.e., divinity, out of one's human nature with God's help, *"Deo concedente."*

truth in that which has always and everywhere been believed and accepted.[135] This canon of orthodoxy was coined by Vincent of Lerins in the course of the early Christian debate over the nature of grace and its relation to free will.

In his appropriation of the Vincentian Canon, Jung's intent is to identify a universally operative process of maturation which expresses itself in a variety of discernibly similar symbols. But he confuses the issue and violates some of his own more mature formulations when he states that these symbols are the "same or very similar"[136] throughout human experience. In one rather loose remark he refers to "the truly amazing phenomenon that certain motifs from myths and legends repeat themselves the world over in identical forms."[137]

Such statements were to force Jung to deny that archetypal theory had anything to do with "innate ideas" and to distinguish more clearly the symbolic expression from its archetypal origin in what he occasionally termed the "collective a priori beneath the personal psyche."[138] This a priori structure of the psyche would be the basis of its "objectivity," in that it would be universal and generative of the world's myriad symbol systems. The problem of formulating the difference between a single generative source giving rise to similar but different symbolic expressions across cultures eventuated in Jung's understanding of the archetype as "psychoid." By this term Jung sought to describe the archetype as an embodied power unknowable in itself yet generative of varied symbols which bore a certain similarity.[139]

Some of these formulations of Jung's could give to archetypal processes a mechanistic quality which misses the subtle but crucial dialectic between the archetype and its various expressions, no one of which ex-

---

135. See "A Psychological Approach to the Dogma of the Trinity," *Psychology and Religion,* CW 11, par. 178. Jung writes, "The archetype is 'that which is believed, always, everywhere and by everybody.' " In "Psychology and Religion," ibid., par. 146, he applies the canon of universality to the Christ figure, and in par. 5 he refers to the spontaneous generation of archetypal symbols.
136. "Concerning Mandala Symbolism," *The Archetypes and the Collective Unconscious,* CW 9i, par. 711.
137. *Two Essays in Analytical Psychology,* CW 7, par. 101.
138. *Memories, Dreams, Reflections,* p. 161. For a typical reference to the a priori and psychoid nature of the collective unconscious, see "On Synchronicity: An Acausal Connecting Principle," *The Structure and Dynamics of the Psyche,* CW 8, par. 962.
139. Ibid., par. 840.

hausts the potential of its archetypal ground. Some modifiers of those passages in which he indicates that archetypal expressions are the same or identical in their conscious manifestations, even cross culturally, suggest that he meant this only in relation to certain set symbols and rituals of a given area at a given time.

For instance, he might legitimately say that Mithraic and Christian baptismal or water purification rites, as well as Eucharistic celebrations, were the same or nearly so along the Mediterranean shores in a variety of Mediterranean cultures at the time that both religions burst into existence. To go beyond this level of observation and to argue that baptismal or Eucharistic rites are always and everywhere accepted by everyone as the only symbols of death and rebirth, or that God-eating is the only rite of becoming divine, is unacceptable. The therapeutic equivalent of such reductionism would be to read dreams as if the symbols that appeared in them had a quantifiable meaning.

Such a mechanistic approach remains wholly insensitive to the radical dialectic at the heart of archetypal theory. Truly significant archetypal expressions have a basis in the collective unconscious, which creates consciousness as that only locus in which it can and must express its archetypal possibilities. This understanding of the living psyche establishes an organic connectedness between the unconscious and consciousness as the precondition for archetypal and religious experience. But if the process is not to be stalled, it must be clearly understood that no particular expression and perhaps no sum total of them can ever exhaust the fecundity of the archetype.

In this precise sense Jung's understanding of the religious psyche is vested with its own iconoclastic principle. On the personal level it would mean that in a healthy psyche no one ever dreams the definitive dream that would obviate the need for further dreams. Rather Jung would have it that every dream is to be interpreted by subsequent dreams in a never-ending process. In this manner, the dreamer is lead to more intensive appropriations of the Self over the course of a lifetime. This understanding of the psyche is behind Jung's hermeneutic derived in part from the wisdom of the Talmud: "The dream is its own interpretation."[140]

In the context of this citation Jung uses the Talmud against Freud to argue that the dream states its truth in undisguised but symbolic discourse.

---

140. "Psychology and Religion," *Psychology and Religion,* CW 11, par. 41.

No deliberately disguised message need be decoded. Rather the interpreter must learn symbolic language, the self's native tongue as maker of dreams and sender of revelations. This interpretative perspective extends also to the reading of dream sequences as the heart of the analytic process. Such a principle of interpretation becomes the basis of the Jungian imperative that the symbol should be allowed to interpret the symbol, that is, that next week's dream be allowed and expected to interpret tonight's.

Where a dream seems merely to repeat itself without alteration, something is stuck in the psyche. The congealment may result from a profound trauma which the psyche cannot as yet integrate, as in the case of shell shock or its equivalents. Or, more commonly in therapeutic experience, the repeating dream may simply indicate that consciousness has not yet assimilated what the Self is saying. Here the implication is that the appropriation by consciousness of the point of the repeating dream is something that must be done as a condition for moving beyond the difficulty the dream highlights.

The same principles can equally well be applied to those collective dreams called religions, usually dreamt by an individual called a messiah, prophet or founder. The redeemer's personal dream becomes a collective religion or societal myth because it embodies the precisely needed compensation proffered by the collective unconscious through the individual messiah to the broader community.

For Jung, all such revelations have a common source. But just as no dream is definitive, so is no religion definitive. Where one was presented as definitive, or even nearly so, one would look to see what archetypal energies such a religion could incorporate only with difficulty. One would look to these energies as the forces that would eventually supplant it, again in the power of a religious myth or with energies that would be the functional equivalent of a religion. If religions could be seen in this light as helpful but destined to be supplanted by the archetypal energies that produced them in the interests of human wholeness, they would lose their tendency to congeal into competing and dangerous absolutes. The perception of their partiality would then welcome rather than block their supercession toward a myth encompassing a broader range of archetypal truth.

Such a perception, at once appreciative and undermining, would make the likelihood of any single redemptive figure ushering in the eschatological kingdom rather remote. But it would give reflective humanity some much-needed time to question the value of such exclusivist and ultimately self-serving eschatological temptations, to perceive their antisocial character, and to surface a more inclusive myth better serving our survival.

Relativization

The dialogue between the universal and the relative in Jung's archetypal theory is crucial to his appreciation of all religions and his denial of the claim to ultimacy by any of them. Jung indeed wants to affirm that a universal ground produces archetypal expressions, such as the religions, whose grasp can be understandably absolute on those possessed by them. Thus he writes: "[The *numinosum*] seizes and controls the human subject, who is always rather its victim than its creator."[141] In theologies unaware of the unconscious the intractability of this grasp is called faith.

With the debilitating effect it has on critical consciousness, how then can the agency which creates faith, and especially communal faith, be understood as friendly to humanity? Jung is very aware of the dangers. Faith in the form of archetypal possession makes of its victim, "an unconscious instrument of the wholesale murderer in man."[142]

It is precisely this threat, identified as the power of archetypal possession, that Jung's psychology battles through the fostering of a conscious dialogue between the ego and archetypal energies. Thus Jung is aware both of the inevitable threat of loss of consciousness to unconscious energies, that is, to the deities, but equally aware that the ego can enter into a conscious dialogue with them, which would at least minimize their threat to conscious autonomy and hopefully recruit them as agents of a more conscious and benign humanity. Indeed, his psychology suggests rather strongly that the Self, in presiding over this dialogue, seeks a consciousness rendered all the more autonomous, vital and balanced because of its cooperation with the Gods seeking incarnation.

Understanding the psyche in this sense shows the inevitability of religion and, by relativizing its manifestations, contributes to making it a safer energy. For no matter how compelling the archetypal grasp of any religious or political faith may be, Jung's psychology holds out to its victims the liberating hope of loss of faith by identifying the archetypal basis of its grip and in so doing loosening it. In this manner his psychology relativizes

---

141. Ibid., par. 6.
142. Ibid., par. 86.

such faith as but one expression of whatever energy and value it may convey and relativizes it also by relating it to equally important countering values. Seen in this light any faith is susceptible to transcendence by the power that gives birth to it. Thus to give an unqualified adherence to one religion as exhaustively meeting humanity's religious possibilities would be as great an affront to maturity as to spend a lifetime under the constrictive tyranny of one dream.

The intersection of universality and relativity in Jung's archetypal theory can be either liberating or abrasive. For it implies that the universal ground of all revelations sponsors them in the service of potential human wholeness. Thus the Christian revelation, for instance, which originally compensated collective consciousness with a much-needed spirituality, might itself become a block to a subsequent balance. In fact Jung did understand the unconscious currently to be working toward such a transcending myth in Christian culture. He more than suggests this in a long letter to Victor White when he writes, "Christ is still the valid symbol. Only God himself can 'invalidate' him through the Paraclete."[143] The obvious implication is that the same Spirit which created the symbol of Christ now urges its completion and so "invalidation."

For the psyche possessed by, and wholly invested in, the Christian myth, participation in such liberating newness could only be experienced as a loss of faith. Much of the pain in current Christian suffering, where it is consciously undergone, is in the conflict between a myth currently experienced as constrictive and a myth yet to be fully imaged. The symbol that would unite the Christian past with the human future has yet to be found. The search for it remains the ultimate threat to the believer and the ultimate freeing hope for those who experience its early promise. Many of the latter hope for a more expansive religious consciousness while continuing to find aspects of their current religiosity somehow sustaining. Jung understands suffering to be nondefeating and truly maturing when born by those suspended between legitimate opposites. Thus the pain of the many who have seen through the limitations of their religious myth and have yet to formulate and fully enter the superseding myth might well constitute a truly redemptive form of suffering.

The move toward a fuller articulation of the Christian myth is helped by

---

143. *C. G. Jung Letters*, vol. 2, letter to Father Victor White, November 24, 1953, p. 138.

the effective blend of the sacramental and iconoclastic in Jung's psychology. His synthesis of these conflicting elements is not unlike the way Paul Tillich combines Catholic substance, the sacramental, with Protestant principle, the iconoclastic, in his own understanding of religious humanity.[144] Jung, like Tillich, would understand all religious experience to derive from a common ground. The experienced power of this ground is the basis of the inevitable sacramental sense in humanity universally. To a great extent Jung would share Tillich's fear of idolatry, the absolute identification of the divine with that through which it appears. As suggested above, such idolatry for Jung would consist in making one dream or religion normative as divinity's exhaustive manifestation. But unlike Tillich, Jung's bent is to view the psyche as doubting the kind of assertion that Tillich makes in spite of his fear of idolatry, namely, that one among the many revelations is somehow final. In light of Jung's understanding of the psyche, any claim to exhaustive possession of a saving truth constricts personal development and is currently a, if not *the*, major threat to human survival.

The above conclusion follows from Jung's attribution of a certain unbounded expressive capacity to archetypal energy, even in its role as creator of religion. Such boundless fecundity makes it likely that archetypal energies need a potentially infinite number of historical expressions to give the archetype adequate conscious realization. Considering the interplay between possibly infinite archetypal creativity and limited human receptivity, our current religions may be preliminary expressions of that which gives rise to them but now may be urging them to go beyond themselves. To hold any as exhaustive would run the risk of an idolatrous truncation of consciousness and aborting the process of the mutual redemption of divinity and humanity which Jung posits as the ground movement in the psyche's creation of history. Thus the very fecundity of the archetypal is the basis of the iconoclastic dimension of Jung's understanding of the psyche, even as the archetypal makes the sense of the sacred and sacramental an experience humanity cannot escape.

Religiously, the threat of absolute but partial conviction is most obvious in that line of religious development which culminates in the monotheisms. Currently the world observes three one-and-only Gods glaring at each other through the eyes of the extensive communities they bond as their

---

144. See, for instance, Paul Tillich, "The Permanent Significance of the Catholic Church for Protestantism" *Protestant Digest*, III (Summer, 1941), pp. 23-41.

chosen. When these communities intersect geographically, the media report the attendant carnage on a daily basis. From a Jungian perspective the hatred bred between competing religious absolutes congealed into human communities is not accidental or peripheral to their bonding faith and professed universal love. Rather this shadow of hate attaches to professed universal love for a number of reasons. Such absolute faith is grounded on archetypal possession, individually and collectively. Were such possession to be broken, the community of the possessed would be broken with it in a relativism that would be experienced as a loss of faith and betrayal of God and tradition by those dependent on their collective unconsciousness for spiritual and sometimes physical security.

Such bonding faith by its very nature cannot tolerate contradiction any more than it can tolerate the suggestion that it shares a common generative ground with other faiths. As Jung pointed out in his debate with Buber, Yahweh is not Allah and neither is God the Father in the Christian Trinity, nor do these aforementioned deities have much in common with Eastern Gods and Goddesses.[145] Yet all are invested with a sense of an exclusive ultimacy, muted though this can be in the Eastern traditions.

When one absolute faith intersects historically and geographically with another, scapegoating ensues. Scapegoat psychology brands the faithless as demonic. Demonized, the infidel can be exterminated in the name of God. Religious slurs cast by one faith on another should be carefully examined by those who cast them. From a Jungian perspective they are externalizations of the unconscious negative evaluations of the believer's own tradition, the collective shadow projected onto the nonconforming individual or group. The dynamic of projecting the collective shadow onto the other at least raises the question as to whether archetypally bonded communities can avoid such projection because it is so endemic to the process that holds them together. To date few historical instances of religious-political bonding provide the basis for a hopeful attitude to the problem, so inevitable is the need to project the collective shadow. Others are now beginning to recognize this social peril and to describe it well as "a collective scapegoat pathology that threatens the survival of our earth."[146]

Applied to the shadow side of Western religious history, Jungian per-

---

145. "Religion and Psychology: A Reply to Martin Buber," *The Symbolic Life,* CW 18, par. 1507.
146. Sylvia Brinton Perera, *The Scapegoat Complex: Toward a Mythology of Shadow and Guilt* (Toronto: Inner City Books, 1986), p. 7.

false religion

spectives on this matter should enable the Christian to see that, for instance, anti-Semitism is not peripheral to that tradition but a natural outgrowth of its monotheistic impulse to bond under the aegis of a one and only God. Beyond the specifically Christian ambit, this insight would help those concerned with peace in religiously troubled areas of the world toward the stark realization that political-economic-military arrangements to relieve such strife are no more than provisional measures doomed to failure. Only the loss of the bonding faith of the conflicted communities will in the end bring any true peace. But loss of faith cannot be legislated. Nor can it begin anywhere else than at home. In the face of a history of faith-induced violence, the loss of faith and the communal "protection" such faith provides would seem as unlikely, indeed foolish, to believers as would unilateral disarmament to the cold warrior.

Confronted by the evil of archetypally induced faith and its dubious bonding, one must ask if Jung's theory can do more than document the impossibility of moving beyond the tragedy of unconscious communities impelled to mutual destruction. Does Jung's understanding of the psyche's resources leave humanity with an impressive psychological documentation of its drive toward self-destruction, but do little to reverse it?

The difficulty is magnified by Jung's own position when he argues consistently that only the individual carries consciousness and, by implication, that newer myths can only be born through individuals responding to the need for such birth. What possibility is there for a renewed consciousness in those born into centuries of faith-induced hatred and loss of life? Would not their birth into the shadow of such murderous faiths simply perpetuate the shadow? It is in asking this question that the true power of what Jung calls the Self would be most severely scrutinized. Is there a power which humanity can access which has, no doubt, created the lesser Gods now authoring religious conflict but which is, perhaps, working through them to a sense of divinity which would alleviate these frictions?

The answer is of vast importance. If it is no, then current provisional political solutions to religious conflict, even if continued indefinitely, will have to suffice. In the face of the intractable nature of the faith divisions which they address, these efforts can only come to be informed with an increasing and abiding sense of the defeat and fragmentation of the human spirit by its own religious aspirations. If the answer is yes, then the current situation can be reimagined as one in which the power that has admittedly authored deficient Gods can raise from the ashes of their followers the

hope of a more encompassing human empathy. And such a hope is not totally without precedent.

If we turn to modern Western development, we may see an instance of
the power of the Self working a consciousness which is both the fruit of,
yet higher than, the religious conflicts that gave rise to it. The murderous
consequences of faiths in conflict was seen through and intellectually and
legally dismantled in the West in that movement called the Enlightenment,
culminating in the French and American Revolutions. It is interesting to
note that one of the forces leading to the prominence of reason were the
intra-Christian religious wars following the Reformation and the dubious
alignment of official religion with *l'ancien regime* in France and elsewhere
at the time of the Revolution. In the face of such conflict and injustice, it
became obvious to the European spirit that the faiths of the militant Reform
and equally militant Romanism could not provide for the humane future of
European civilization. Reason emerged as a saving power vested with a
vision that transcended that of the conflicting religious powers it displaced.

The paradoxical deification of reason as a power which transcended the
religious narrowness of the disputants no doubt contributed much to the
resolution of the strife, but did not and could not extinguish the archetypal
powers which breed political and religious commitment, and so conflict.
As Jung often points out, the energies which create religion and its convictions did not evaporate with the Enlightenment's new perspective. Rather
these energies were transformed from religious into political form, into
those "isms" whose archetypal bonding continues to divest their victims of
both intellectual autonomy and broader humane sympathies.[147]

Operating in political guise, these archetypal energies continued their al-
liance with death in the making of political faiths, those conflicting absolutes which have made the twentieth century one of politically acceptable
genocide. The symbols may vary but the loss of life continues, made more
efficient by technological advances in killing. The most recent and undeniable instance of archetypally inspired mass murder was the sacrifice of two
hundred thousand lives, a conservative estimate, to the archetypal image of
a "New World Order." So complete was the unconsciousness surrounding
this act of genocide that its perpetrators were welcomed home as heroes,
completing the archetypal enactment with the same ritual once performed

---

147. See my discussion of this aspect of Jung's psychology in *The Illness That
We Are,* pp. 37-38.

by Roman Emperors parading their victims and loot through the streets of Rome to the cheers of the mob.

A further disturbing feature these contemporary political faiths share with their religious forebears is their apocalypticism. A foundational element in Jung's psychology would insist that personal growth and collective survival are worked through processes in which absolute opposites are differentiated in the service of higher syntheses. The main target of Jung's criticism of apocalyptic consciousness is its refusal of this task and with it the mature expansiveness that growth demands and brings. In its place the apocalyptic mind seizes on its own religious partiality based on a one-sided perception of a God in whom there is no darkness. Unaware of its own and of divinity's shadow, the apocalyptic mind is imbued with a righteousness and truth incapable of perceiving such qualities in others, onto whom it too often projects its own and divinity's shadow.[148] The opponent becomes the demon who, rather than contributing to one's own totality through the painful processes of integration, is cast into the sea of living fire.

This process is but a variation of the demonization which seeks the contradicting other's destruction. Far from being confined to Biblical fundamentalism, this apocalypticism informs twentieth-century political power. Thus in the eighties, talk of the "evil empire" and of one's political opponent as "Satan" was on the lips of world leaders. More recently, in preparation for genocide in the Gulf, the opponent was branded in Western legislative assemblies and in the media as "absolute evil."

This historical foray brings us back to the question of the practical utility of Jung's conception of the Self as a power which moves history toward more inclusive states of consciousness, though always working through individual consciousness caught in some form of history's archetypal contradictions. If the Self was operative in surfacing the myth of reason in the face of post-Reformation religious intransigence, can it now work the alleviation of equally powerful conflicting energies in their current political dress?

If one argues that it can, then the fostering of processes of individuation and the more inclusive sensitivities accompanying them, far from being solipsistic, have both political and social import. Jung's endorsement of

---

148. See "Answer to Job," *Psychology and Religion,* CW 11, pars. 729-744, for the substance of Jung's critique of apocalypticism, especially as found in the Book of Revelation.

the individual's conscious conversation with the unconscious would then become a survival strategy in that it holds out the potential for a myth or faith transcending current truncated commitments, much as reason transcended disruptive religious disputes at the time of the Enlightenment.

Because of its political and social value, then, Jung's so-called gnosticism should be reexamined against the claims of those who would brand it and all gnostic consciousness as apolitical or as its opposite, totalitarian. It is a strange paradox that such opposite charges can be leveled at a gnostic sensibility. The basis for the charge of gnosticism as a form of apolitical solipsism is hardly applicable to Jung's psychology, which would work to make the individual aware of the numinous or addictive basis in the psyche for total political or religious commitment of any stripe. This side of Jung is the ultimate defense against any kind of totalitarianism, for conscious dialogue with the unconscious would alert the prospective political or religious convert to the truncating nature of an absolute commitment to anything. With the resource of Jungian psychology, the individual would thus be less susceptible to psychic manipulation by either religious or political prophets and, at the same time, well equipped to give a measured response to their partial truth. Such wise reserve, if widespread, would undermine any tyranny still able to muster the masses to kill for its truth.

The anti-gnostic, persuaded that at least Jung's brand of gnosticism is not without survival value and so of political consequence, can then swing to the opposite pole and argue that gnosticism inevitably leads to totalitarianism. Here the argument is more complex when put into the context of recent Western history. Jacob Boehme (1575-1624), a Christian mystic or gnostic much admired and cited by Jung, was perhaps the first shaper of contemporary Western consciousness to undergo an experience of divinity which, when reflected on, implied rather strongly that a very vital and conflicted creator sought some sort of resolution of divine suffering in history.[149] That such resolution was historically imminent grounds the profound hope and energy that characterize Boehme's volatile opus.

Hegel saw that Boehme's experience centered on a radical revisioning of the divine-human relation around the issue of the meaning of historical

---

149. There is an excellent treatment of this aspect of Boehme's mysticism in David Walsh, *The Mysticism of Innerworldly Fulfillment: A Study of Jacob Boehme* (Gainesville: University of Florida Press, 1983). Walsh's exposition, though sensitive and accurate, remains uneasy with the social-political implications of Boehme's thought.

consciousness and its development in marked tension with the theological tradition of a wholly self-sufficient God to whom creation remained an afterthought. Hegel realized that Boehme's experience was of such intensity that it could only find expression in the "wild and fanciful"[150] outpouring of imagery that so characterizes Boehme's work. But Hegel equally well realized that Boehme's experience and the revisioning of the divine-human relationship it implied was the philosophical and theological question of the age.

Indeed, Hegelian scholars describe Hegel's own work as a prolonged effort to give adequate philosophical expression and resolution to Boehme's problematic.[151] Hegel's philosophy, like Jung's psychology, came to the conclusion that history is the process of God's self-completion through the resolution of the divine antinomy in historical human conflict. Thus Hegel sees in history the same process that Jung locates in the psyche: the resolution in historical human consciousness of a self-contradiction that remained beyond resolution in divinity.

The potential for totalitarianism and an offensive millennialism in such perspectives arise from the initial intensity of Boehme's visionary experience, Hegel's clarifying formulation of it, and Marx's transformation of the idea that divinity can and must become real only in history, into a political program destined to culminate in a consciousness of universal human communion. To the extent that these archetypally inspired religious and political ideas can so possess the mind, they do indeed provide the psychic basis for totalitarianism. As such they lend credence to Jung's contention that the murderous potential intrinsic to religion has in our century taken on political form. But Jung's gnosticism, rather than endorse such totalitarianism, can both show its basis in the psyche and point to its more positive side in the native teleology of the psyche toward the sense of unity, while providing humanity with the defense against its literalization and implementation in religious or political programs.

It is all too strange then to hear Christian protagonists inveighing

---

150. G. Hegel, *Lectures on the Philosophy of Religion,* ed. P.C. Hodgson (Berkeley: University of California Press, 1985), vol. 3, p. 289. See also Hegel's references to Boehme, ibid., pp. 200, 293-294; and the discussion of the Boehme-Hegel relation in Tom Darby, *The Feast: Meditations on Politics and Time* (Toronto: University of Toronto Press, 1982), pp. 122-129 and appendix 1, pp. 154-155.

151. See references in Darby, *The Feast,* where this position is cited as that of A. Koyre (p. 123).

against both gnosticism itself and its Jungian variant,[152] since the original Christian experience was itself an unconscious apocalyptic experience. If anything, in Jung's estimate, apocalyptic consciousness falls short of gnosticism in its unconscious identification with the bright side of the unconscious. This one-sidedness grounds the refusal of the apocalyptic mind to address the opposites of good and evil in God. But it is precisely this more encompassing aspect of the gnostic myth that makes it a currently safer political myth, since it is imbued with a deep sense of the need to unite rather than exorcise opposites, all of which are God grounded. Thus the potentially terminal conviction that the world is soon to end in a somewhat unilateral triumph of good over evil, the essence of apocalypticism, is countered by a gnostic sensitivity that since the opposites are present in God as creator they should be included in creation's completion.

In fact, in a conscious gnostic dialectic this experience of the light and pure side of divinity, or, more precisely, of a dimension of divinity beyond good and evil, is the foundational experience which enables and demands the gnostic's awareness of the shadow side of both existence and of its creator. Far from being a life-denying position, gnosticism is critical of the distortions of existence because of a deeper sense of goodness. This sense of the wellsprings of joy in the depths of life is the essential dimension of being which Tillich rightly says is implicit in the most somber analyses of life's existential distortions. It is this point that Hans Jonas's equation of gnosticism with a negative existentialism or, worse, fatalism, seems largely to have missed.[153]

Jonas's valuable commentary is too complex to address at length but the dualism which supposedly exists between the individual gnostic and his Spirit-inspired gnosis, on one side, and nature on the other, could be countered even in Jonas's own terms had he dwelt on his own formulation of gnostic "dualism" as "the immanent experience of a disunion of man and world as from its psychological ground."[154] Then the nondualistic and organic nature of gnosticism could be exploited, as Jung does in his

---

152. See, as typical, Christopher Lasch, "Anti-modern Mysticism: E.M. Cioran & C.G. Jung," *New Oxford Review*, vol. 58, no. 2 (March 1991), pp. 20f. Lasch restates the substance of Buber's charges against Jung's gnosticism. As a committed Christian he is uncomfortable with the relativity of the psyche and what it would do to absolute faith in Christianity.

153. See *The Gnostic Religion* (Boston: Beacon Press, 1958), esp. "Epilogue: Gnosticism, Nihilism and Existentialism," pp. 320ff.

154. Ibid., p. 326.

understanding of the gnostic as working the realization of an ever-present potential unity with this one ground of mind and nature.

Other modern commentators, such as Elaine Pagels, are able to understand gnosticism in this way, and more, to link it, as does Jung, to Christian mysticism through Eckhart. Here the idea would be that unity with one's natural divinity is the truth of Eden symbolism which depicts God, humanity and nature as transparent to each other. Moreover, Pagels, like Jung, refers to this gnostic-mystical consciousness not as something lost in the past and inaccessible in the present but as "a spiritual potential latent in the human psyche."[155]

In the end, by raising gnostic experience to full consciousness and exposing its psychological dynamic, Jung shows that apocalypticism, a sister experience, is in and of itself an immature and dangerous response to social conflict, working to eternalize rather than synthesize the contradiction in divinity and humanity.

At the more personal level, Jung argues that what the Christ figure lacks as an image of the Self, current gnostic experience could complement in a safer and more complete consciousness, again, never divested of social import.[156] Indeed, Jung proposes a recovery of a gnostic sense in the interests of restoring religious experience to the Christian deprived of it through centuries of Christian theologies. A gnostic sensitivity, he suggests, could thus "serve many people today as a bridge to a more living appreciation of Christian tradition."[157] Rather than see gnosticism as a heresy hostile to Christianity, Jung would reverse this perspective and see Christianity as a heresy hostile to religious experience itself and to the primordial gnostic understanding of humanity's movement toward that communion with the totality that a healthy religiosity should breed.

Again in his appreciation of gnosticism one sees the social, even apologetic, concern in Jung's life and work. For instance, he criticizes Albert Schweitzer not for undermining the then literal understanding of Christian Biblical literature by showing it to be a document of excited apocalyptic imagination; rather he is critical of Schweitzer for abandoning a believing community, whose literal-historical faith his scholarship had helped destroy, without a replacement and then leaving the European victims of the

---

155. *Adam, Eve and the Serpent* (New York, Random House, 1988), p. 65.
156. See "Christ a Symbol of the Self," *Aion*, CW 9ii, par. 76.
157. "Transformation Symbolism in the Mass," *Psychology and Religion,* CW 11, par. 444.

resultant spiritual vacuum to the psychologist.[158] Put in this context, Jung's critique of apocalypticism and his appreciation of conscious gnosticism work to provide the dispossessed Christian with access to the energies of the Self in the wake of the corrosion of Biblical literalism. The gnostic experience of the Self could enhance the power of Biblical symbolism in the wake of its historical discrediting, while warning believers of the capacity of archetypal experience to render dangerously unconscious those uncritically possessed by it.

In light of these reflections it becomes obvious that much of the thrust of those who would try to discredit Jung as a gnostic, and associate him with the less attractive sides of the New Age movement, are defending a literal Christianity taken as a normative and final religious expression. They are frightened of the implication in Jung's thought that the unconscious currently works toward an appreciative undermining and surpassing of their cherished myth. In the end they are afraid of immediate experience of the unconscious, preferring an institutional mediation that makes religion available and dependable but very tame, and, to ever-increasing numbers, simply unintelligible. This kind of criticism would remain insensitive even to Paul Tillich's suggestion that orthodox Christianity needs a new gnosis in the interest of its own revitalization.[159] There is no need for such religious revitalization in those who have found "the real thing."[160] Should the "real thing" be an advertisement for the superiority of one soft drink over its competitors, it might be acceptable. As an endorsement of one revelation against many, it speaks of a religiosity whose spiritual maturity is not far removed from Madison Avenue.

But as such truncated faith in fact constellates in the contemporary world, the question arises, "What prophylactic do we have to prevent such

---

158. See *C. G. Jung Letters*, vol. 2, letter to Pastor Walter Uhsadel, February 6, 1952, pp. 39-40; letter to Dr. Dorothea Hoch, September 23, 1952, p. 85; letter to Carlton Smith, September 9, 1953, p. 125; and esp. letters to Pastor Willi Bremi, December 11, 1953, pp. 140-143 and December 26, 1953, pp. 144-145.
159. P. Tillich, *Systematic Theology*, vol. 1 (Chicago: University of Chicago Press, 1951), pp. 95-96, 153-154. Here Tillich refers to a gnosis which engages the individual totally as a consequence of a conscious inhesion in the essential. In this sense it is related to his understanding of *amor intellectualis*.
160. See Christopher Lasch, "The New Age Movement: No effort, No Truth, No Solutions," *New Oxford Review*, vol. 58, no. 3 (April 1991), p. 13. Lasch concludes his rejection of the gnosticism of the New Age, which he uncritically and unappreciatively extends to include Jung's psychology, with the sentence, "The only corrective of the ersatz religions of the New Age is to turn to the real thing."

dubious fecundation of our minds by such contending and murderous Gods?" And then: "How might we lose our lesser faiths for a safer, more encompassing one?"

The thrust of a Jungian response would lie in the cultivation of that consciousness engendered by the process of individuation itself. Put succinctly, this would mean that an increasing number of individuals would become aware that in the depths of their interiority they intersect with the universal ground of all mythologies and that this experience both illuminates and relativizes the myths, religious and political, into which they have been born. This formulation respects Jung's insistence that only the individual is the bearer of consciousness.

Should a sense of the necessarily variegated appearance of the sacred in human history gain widespread acceptance, the ability of religious or political leaders to commit physical or spiritual atrocities would decrease because the collective unconsciousness needed for such crime would be directly and proportionately attenuated. Increasingly widespread circles of consciousness would be more comfortable with a sensitivity that the ground with which they are in immediate communion might need some endless number of religious expressions and an unknowable number of aeons to bring itself to full consciousness in humanity. Religious commitment would no longer need to be exclusive and prone to lethal fanaticism.

Jung describes the task of the redemption of divinity in terms of the evolution of religious consciousness when he summarizes its history with the statement that the many Gods became one and the one God became human.[161] The deities went through these phases because it was only in human consciousness, initially projecting many Gods, that they could recognize themselves. The movement to their unity and humanization was inevitable with the withdrawal of the projections that had created them. The question now is whether humanity is up to this continued interiorization of the divinities which stand so ready to destroy it if left in projection.

The question can be restated along these lines. Jung shows more clearly and convincingly than most the paradox of the inevitability of religion and its shadow side, the death that seems inevitably to follow in its wake. What is his resolution to the dilemma of the tragedy and possibility that humanity's inescapable religious nature poses? Jung's answer was that these competing deities originate in the human psyche and can become

---

161. "Psychology and Religion," *Psychology and Religion,* CW 11, par. 141.

humanity's resource if consciously faced there. But this would involve a rather sustained dialogue with an inner world on the part of those still fascinated with external reality and deities outside the psyche.

Jung may have died wondering whether humanity had the time and the inclination to survive its faiths through a turn inward which could identify their origin and establish yet again a new testament or covenant with divinity. The hope of the evolution of such a state of consciousness may have informed Jung's late and wistful remark: "[In] the afternoon of humanity, in a distant future . . . even conquest will cease to be a dream."[162]

---

162. "Commentary on 'The Tibetan Book of the Great Liberation,' " *Psychology and Religion*, CW 11, par. 787.

4

Jung and the Christian Spirit:
An Appreciative Undermining

As the previous chapter suggests, Jung's psychology is effectively a countermyth currently in the process of supplanting, even as it appreciates, Christianity and other monotheistic mythologies. As such his psychology is imbued with a spirituality more capable of sacralizing all that is than is the Christian myth.

However, if we are to seek to relate Spirit in the psychology of C.G. Jung to the Christian meaning of Spirit, it would be wise to begin by asking, "What is Spirit?" and "What is spirituality?" These questions might best be answered by looking for a meaning of Spirit that both Christianity and Jung could share, preliminary to a discussion of how they might seriously differ. In the end this will reveal that the Spirit that enlivens Jung's psychology is less than wholly compatible with the Spirit which unites Father and Son eternally, and humanity to both in time, as the Christian myth would have it.

The term "Spirit" in its benign Jungian and Christian sense points to the Spirit (or, with Jung, to the Spirits) of true holiness as the source of those energies that make life worth living and living fully. With this understanding, spirituality becomes the sum total of those processes by which we access the blessed Spirits. From them we receive our libido, that zest for life which enables us not only to survive but to go on with that enthusiasm which, as the etymology of the word suggests, means being in God and experiencing God in ourselves.

Energy or libido in this sense is life. Its surplus is life abundant. As such, the energy that funds a fuller life is humanity's greatest value and the search for it is humanity's abiding concern and ceaseless activity. From Jung's perspective this makes all of human history as well as personal striving a religious quest. For religions themselves are born out of the experience of such primordial energy. Thus they live from their capacity to give to their adherents the energies of the Spirit or Spirits, and they die when they lose this capacity.

The religious mind calls the experience of the energies which make life

75

first possible and then fuller the experience of God. From the viewpoint of a modern psycho-spirituality, then, the accessing of that energy is the business of a working, effective spirituality. Such a spirituality would function to bring our consciousness into living contact with that dimension of our humanity from which its experience of the divine and the grace of being whole naturally arises. *Thus understood, God is our experience of the energy that makes us whole.*

The human being cannot get enough of such energy and the life it funds, nor can God get enough realization in human life thus funded. In Jung's understanding of the psyche, this much-treasured energy or libido which feeds the life of consciousness is lodged in the archetypal dimension of the unconscious. Thus Jung identifies the experience of archetypal energies with the experience of the divine when he writes, for instance, that "in God we honor the energy of the archetype."[163] In this passage, taken from the work that led to Jung's break with Freud, Jung goes on immediately to say that the mystics, and here he cites Mechthilde of Magdeburg and Hildegarde of Bingen, identify archetypal experience and the energy it generates with the experience of being loved by God.[164]

The experience of such energy is thus the experience of God born to consciousness through whatever specific symbol the energy might choose to clothe itself on the occasion of its epiphany. In these passages Jung points to some images which commonly bear this numinous charge, such as the sun, light, fire and parental figures. In Mechthilde's case, he adds that the central symbol bearing the energy of the divine is that of sexual intimacy and physical love-making with a seventeen-year-old lover whom she identified with the youthful Christ.[165] One could hardly propose a more adequate image to depict a woman giving birth to the divine within through union with her divine masculinity.

Thus, both Christian and Jungian spirituality might well agree that the business of spirituality is to make accessible to its practitioners the energies that carry us through life with a sense of being in God and of living out of those divine energies that entice and propel us to become whole. Both

---

163. *Symbols of Transformation*, CW 5, par. 135.
164. Ibid., pars. 136-139.
165. See Mechthilde of Magdeburg, *The Flowing Light of the Godhead*, trans. Lucy Menzies (London: Longmans, Green, 1953), book 1, section 44, and my essay "Love, Celibacy and the Inner Marriage: Jung and Mechthilde of Magdeburg," in *Love, Celibacy and the Inner Marriage*, pp. 25-43.

might further agree that to the extent we become whole, we more truly realize our nature as it images God, and that in some sense God becomes more real through that imaging in our humanity. At yet another and deeper level, they might agree that the life-giving and whole-making Spirit, a truly Holy Spirit, works to unite opposites in divine life and in human life. This makes of the Holy Spirit what Jung, some mystics and the alchemists call a *coincidentia oppositorum*, a living coincidence of opposites. And here the plot thickens considerably. For the idea of the Holy Spirit as that power which unites the opposites in divine and human life makes of it a power which paradoxically works a unity of conflicting opposites and is itself the fruit or child of their union.

This point is made explicitly by the medieval theologian and doctor of the Catholic Church, St. Bonaventure, who describes the Holy Spirit as the bond which unites Father and Son, but also as the fruit of their union.[166] Jung makes an identical point in his work on the Mass. Borrowing from alchemical imagery he argues that the Self in bringing about the union of ego and unconscious is born into consciousness or becomes incarnate as a child of the very union it works.[167]

Though they share a vision of the paradox that the Spirit is born from the unities it works, it is at this point that the Christian understanding of Spirit and the Spirit of Jung's psychology begin to diverge over the crucial point of how the Spirit of God relates to the Spirit of humanity, and what the nature of that relationship is. This first point of tension is foundational. It centers on how the Christian and the Jungian traditions understand God, as the source of life's energies and unifier of its opposites, to be present to humanity.

A second point of tension addresses the question of how the two traditions understand God's life to be self-sufficient in its own right, and what consequences this has for the valuation of creation and the role of human consciousness in it.

A third point of tension lies in the motivation that each tradition attributes to God in creating and in entering creation in an incarnation un-

---

166. See my *Paul Tillich and Bonaventure: An Evaluation of Tillich's Claim to Stand in the Augustinian-Franciscan Tradition* (Leiden: E.J. Brill, 1975), pp. 125f.
167. See, for instance, the key passage in "Transformation Symbolism in the Mass," *Psychology and Religion,* CW 11, par. 400, where Jung argues that the Self gives rise to consciousness and then seeks to become real in its child through human cooperation with its importunities.

derstood as a discrete, historical intervention into an already existing order. Differences in evaluating divine motivation lead again to significant differences in the understanding of creaturehood and the creature's role as a participant in processes of redemption.

A fourth point is closely related to the third. It asks whether the Christian God, the Trinity, allegedly the creator of all, can really encompass all that is, and, if not, where did the rest of reality come from?

In most orthodox Christian traditions God is understood to be, at least potentially, wholly other than creation and human consciousness. This is the basic meaning of what theologians term "divine transcendence." If one unpacks the imagination which accompanies this understanding, it implies that God is eternally self-sufficient and in no need of humanity. Creation is a distinct and secondary act and in no way necessitated by the dynamics of divine life itself. Creation then becomes an unforced act of grace. However, because it is a grace divested of any divine need, such a conception of creation carries with it overtones of the gratuitous approaching the arbitrary.

Such arbitrariness became a deeply abrasive aspect of the Christian myth to such Christian thinkers as Teilhard de Chardin. His science enabled him to understand how in fact God had created through the evolutionary process. The process was one of trial and error deeply imbued with effort, loss and suffering, which Teilhard understood, much like Jung, to be continuing through its human layer toward the completion of God in a final pleroma, his point Omega. From his perspective, then, the attribution of arbitrariness to divine creativity was not only ignorant of how humanity had in fact come about, but also remained insensitive to the divine compulsion to create in order to become complete in creation.

Worse, such theological imagination remained wholly impervious to the deeper meaning of human suffering, whose sole dignity and justification lies in the eventual mutual completion of humanity and divinity. The theological imagination attaching to a self-sufficient deity arbitrarily creating would thus hold in contempt the meaning of human suffering, and emasculate human efforts to move toward unity.

If one traces the logical unfolding of this theological stance, it follows that just as God had no compulsion to create, he had no compulsion to redeem humanity when it fell in the sin of Adam, nor any reason to be diminished if the cosmos terminates in eternally divided communities of the saved and the damned, as apocalyptic imagination would have it. In this vision God, at least in principle, remains external to the individual and to the human psyche. Access to God, imagined in this way, usually involves God's graceful and, again, totally free initiative in approaching the fallen human. This divine initiative or intrusion is imagined in a variety of ways in Christian traditions.

Thus in the world view of medieval Christianity, still widely operative in contemporary Catholic imagination, a God external to the world creates it without compulsion and after its collective fall sends the Christ figure who redeems it. The redemption is continued in the Church through the sacraments, infusing a new life of grace into the soul and new capacities into the intellect and will. These faculties now have God as their object through the newly acquired theological virtues of faith, hope and charity. This is the position of Aquinas, the Aristotelian, and while Bonaventure, Aquinas's Platonic contemporary, understands a more immediate experience of God in the very fabric of human self-awareness, he, too, grounds his theology on a natural-supernatural split between God and humanity in the economy of grace as the basis of his theology. In the end Bonaventure, like Aquinas, effectively externalizes a self-sufficient God who approaches humanity from beyond and so also adopts the dualism of a supernatural-natural world view.[168]

With the Reformation this externalism remained. The Word of God in Scripture and sermon came to the fore over sacrament and ecclesial hierarchy. The individual was still justified by a faith generated, not out of humanity's experience of its groundedness in God in the here and now, but from participation in the transforming power of the historical Christ figure and/or his heavenly Father. Thus in all major orthodox variants on the motif of justification by faith alone, the Christ figure is understood as external to the psyche, usually as a unique individual in the historical past, acting on behalf of a transcendent God whom humanity can no longer naturally experience in itself due to the obscuring and corrupting power of sin, both original and personal.

This traditional imagining of the relation of the creature to the creator implies that the creature is wholly divested of a natural sense of God. Thus it remains incompatible with Jung's understanding of the soul's natural and universal sense of God grounded on God's native and experiential

---

168. See my *Paul Tillich and Bonaventure,* chapter 1, "Tillich's Evaluation of the Thirteenth Century," pp. 21-50.

presence to the soul. Jung writes of the soul, in opposition to religious views of humanity which cast it as a stranger to the sense of God: "On the contrary it [the soul] has the dignity of an entity endowed with consciousness of a relationship to Deity."[169] He continues:

> At all events the soul must contain in itself the faculty of relationship to God, i.e., a correspondence, otherwise a connection could never come about. *This correspondence is, in psychological terms, the archetype of the God-image.*[170]

In these words it is obvious that Jung means to say that there is a natural connectedness between God and the soul which makes the experience of God a universal human possibility and necessity.

The major thrust of Jung's critique of Christian consciousness lies in his contention that it has lost this sense of God's presence to the soul. Consequently its observances become external to the soul and lose their power to bring the soul into immediate contact with divine energy. He writes about this:

> It may easily happen, therefore, that a Christian who believes in all the sacred figures is still underdeveloped and unchanged in his inmost soul because he has "all God outside" and does not experience him in the soul.[171]

In these passages Jung suggests that the understanding of a God "all outside" is a critique of externalism he shares with Meister Eckhart, the famous and condemned fourteenth-century Dominican monk and mystic.[172] Eckhart describes the culmination of his personal mystical experience as "the breakthrough."[173] In this state, all distinction between himself and the Godhead disappeared and Eckhart fully recovered what had belonged to him from the outset, his natural divinity and eternity. One can hardly think of an experience of God as more intimate to our humanity and more at odds with Karl Barth's conception of a "wholly other" transcendent God. As if he were explicitly denying Barth's notion of God as so

---

169. "Introduction to the Religious and Psychological Problems of Alchemy," *Psychology and Alchemy,* CW 12, par. 11.
170. Ibid., italics in original.
171. Ibid., par. 12.
172. See ibid., par. 10. The link between Jung and Eckhart is discussed at length below, in chapter 6.
173. See Eckhart's sermon, "Blessed Are the Poor," in *Meister Eckhart, Mystic and Philosopher*, trans. and commentary by Reiner Schurmann (Bloomington: Indiana University Press, 1978), pp. 214f. The word "breakthrough" is on p. 219.

wholly beyond the soul, Jung adds in a footnote to a discussion of the
kind of intimacy which Eckhart establishes between God and the soul:

> It is therefore psychologically quite unthinkable for God to be simply the
> "wholly other," for a "wholly other" could never be one of the soul's deep-
> est and closest intimacies—which is precisely what God is.[174]

Indeed, much of Jung's effort as a psychologist concerned with the
state of the human soul was to reconnect the individual Christian, and also
the wider culture, with the natural energies of God in the soul, even
though this reconnection was a heresy to so many theologies uprooted
from humanity's natural sense of God. One can feel Jung's impatience
when he writes of this problem:

> Grace comes from elsewhere; at all events from outside. Every other point
> of view is sheer heresy. Hence it is quite understandable why the human
> psyche is suffering from undervaluation.[175]

This passage reveals Jung's feeling that his efforts to reconnect the soul
with its own divine depths were rarely appreciated and, where understood,
often rejected by orthodoxy as heretical.[176]

Thus the first point of major divergence between the two spiritualities is
the Christian insistence on the possibility of a total discontinuity between a
wholly transcendent God and the human. Effectively this dualism splits the
experience of God from the experience of one's humanity. It was against
this religious perspective that Jung so often insisted that humanity's experience of its depths as they rise to consciousness is the basis of humanity's
ineradicable experience of God.

But there is more to this divergence between Jung and the Christian on
how they imagine Spirit and access to it. And the more centers around the
question of divinity's need to create humanity and human consciousness in
order to relieve itself of a plight beyond its powers of resolution within the
processes of divine life itself. This question introduces the note of necessity into creation, a note which flatly contradicts the traditional Christian
emphasis on creation as an act wholly divested of divine compulsion.

One can appreciate this divergence through using the theology of Paul

---

174. "Introduction to the Religious and Psychological Problems of Alchemy,"
Psychology and Alchemy, par. 11, note 6.
175. "Commentary on 'The Tibetan Book of the Great Liberation,' " *Psychology
and Religion,* CW 11, par. 771.
176. See above, chapter 2.

Tillich as both a Christian theology and one sensitive to Jung's problematic but in the end unable to solve it. Tillich, like Jung, strove mightily throughout his creative life to conceive of the human and divine in patterns of harmonious intersection. He too was aware that when the point of identity between God and humanity is denied, the ability to conceive of the divine-human relation as vested with humanizing potential is lost. In addressing this problem, Tillich built his theology on an idea of God's presence to humanity arguably as equally intimate to the human as is the experience of God to the psyche in Jung's psychology.

For Tillich, God is the ground of human "being and meaning,"[177] the depth of reason[178] and the source of humanity's deepest and most abiding concern, its thirst for the ultimate. Such concern for the ultimate functions for Tillich as the universal basis of faith.[179] This conception of religious humanity denies the possibility of atheism to the individual even as it undermines cultural pretensions to be secular. Writes Tillich on this point, "Secular culture is essentially as impossible as atheism, because both presuppose the unconditional element and both express ultimate concern."[180] Why, then, could one not use Tillich's theological anthropology, so thoroughly imbued with the being and sense of God, as a theological paradigm of the integration of humanity with its native divinity so fully worked in Jung's mature period?[181]

The answer is that such a synthesis cannot be worked, as thoroughly as Jung does, even from Tillich's integrative viewpoint. This is because Tillich and most orthodox Christian theologians share the idea that the opposites in divine life are united eternally by the Spirit as the precondition of creation.[182] Indeed, for many theologians this divine perfection or completion as a living unity of opposites is the substance of the meaning of

---

177. Paul Tillich, *Systematic Theology* (Chicago: University of Chicago Press, 1951-1963), vol. 1, p. 112.

178. Ibid., pp. 79f.

179. Ibid., vol. 3, p. 130: "In a short formula one can say that faith is the state of being grasped by an ultimate concern."

180. *Theology of Culture*, ed. R.C. Kimball (Oxford: Oxford University Press, 1959), p. 27.

181. See my effort to do this in *The Psyche as Sacrament, A Comparative Study of C.G. Jung and Paul Tillich* (Toronto: Inner City Books, 1981), and my rejection of the possibility in "Jung and Tillich Reconsidered," in *Love, Celibacy and the Inner Marriage*, pp. 59ff.

182. See Tillich's statements on the Trinity in *Systematic Theology*, vol. 1, "God as Living," pp. 241-242, and vol. 3, "The Trinitarian Symbols," pp. 283ff.

God as Trinity. Against this widely held orthodox position stands Jung's mature insistence that the source of human consciousness and life could not resolve its self-contradiction in eternity, and so created human consciousness in time as the only place in which the conflict at the heart of divine life could be perceived and potentially resolved.

On this crucial point Tillich and Jung part company, though Tillich, as a Christian theologian, went about as far as he could go. For Tillich understands the Trinity to be a symbol pointing to a split in the divine life healed by the Spirit of God from eternity. Tillich's depictions of the divine splits are impressive. He points to the abyss dimension of God and relates this dimension of deity, in imagery dependent on Jacob Boehme—another of Jung's much admired mystics—to the dark fire, the primordial but unformed energy of the unconscious.[183] The other dimension of the Trinity, in opposition to its primordial depths, is the *logos*, the principle of communication, of form, of the intelligible world both in God's mind and beyond. The Holy Spirit is then the power which unites these eternally conflicting opposites of infinite power and infinite meaning in divine life itself and eternally.[184]

Beyond the Trinity as the ground of created human life and reason, the Spirit works there also to lead human life and consciousness into the integration of all opposites and so into that blessedness of conflict resolved which is the hallmark of Trinitarian life. Thus Tillich's most basic idea is that the Holy Spirit having worked the reconciliation of opposites in divine life from eternity seeks now to lead human life into this integration and wholeness from its active presence in the depths of human life itself.[185]

These positions do indeed strike a certain resonance with the profound structural themes of Jung's later psychology and its spirituality. Yet, as stated, in the end they fall short. One can visualize the shortfall by focusing on Jung's early piece of gnostic poetry, *Seven Sermons to the Dead.*[186] Here he uses a gnostic conception of the initial pleroma, the full-

---

183. See, for instance, Tillich's description of the abyss dimension of deity and its connection to Rudolph Otto's concept of God as *tremendum* in *Systematic Theology*, vol. 1, p. 216. For his description of this dimension of deity in terms reminiscent of Boehme, see ibid., p. 251.
184. Ibid.
185. This integration of opposites by the Spirit in divine and human life is the substance of Tillich's thought on the "Ontological Elements" which structure so much of his system. See *Systematic Theology*, vol. 1, pp. 174-185.
186. *Memories, Dreams, Reflections,* appendix 5, pp. 378ff.

ness of the creative principle, to give poetic expression to what he means by creation.[187] The pleroma contains all that will and can be. However, because this initial fullness is divested of a point of discrimination, or consciousness, all the opposites which are so evident in our experience of everyday life are there but in a contaminated or undifferentiated state. They await the birth of reason's discriminatory power. Thus the creating God, the source of all that can be, awaits and demands the birth of human consciousness before its own unconsciousness can be differentiated and its latent contradictions progressively resolved—in and through human consciousness. This paradigm clearly understands humanity as the sole agent of conscious discrimination in the universe.

These early insights culminate in Jung's "Answer to Job," where he makes it explicit that Job, as representative of developing human religious consciousness, clearly perceives that Yaweh's conflict remains unresolved in Yaweh's life and seeks resolution in Job's.[188] This revisioning of the divine-human relation relocates the meaning of history, both personal and collective, in the suffering human perception of that side of the divine contradiction most painfully evident in communal or individual life. The perception of such suffering thus precedes its resolution with the help of the same divinity that constellates it.

Certain implications accompany this cosmology and its related spirituality, which with difficulty can be assimilated by more traditional Christian world views. First it implies that God as creator has not consciously resolved in a divine life-process independent of humanity's the powerful contradictions that remain unperceived and active in it. Yet this same divine life-process contains within itself a significant resource for the resolution of its conflicts in and through human consciousness. Jung calls this power the Self. In its latent presence in the life of the creator, to put it in a religious idiom, the Self pushes first for the creation of human consciousness and then for the resolution of the conflicted life of the divine unconscious in human consciousness. In this role consciousness functions as both the creature of the Self and collaborator with it in its drive to become incarnate in human consciousness. This process of resolution is one of repeated cyclical immersion or death of conscious life into its divine matrix, followed by successful rebirth from the womb of all consciousness to a more

---

187. Ibid., p. 379.
188. See above, chapter 1.

vigorous engagement with the surrounding world.[189] This ambivalent side of God the creator, as conflicted in its own life and so driven to resolve its conflicts in human life through the power of the Self, is the substance of Jung's assertion that Job "expected help from God against God."[190]

This vision of reality alters the divine-human relation in many ways but especially in what is meant by redemption and morality. Job becomes an image of humanity initially overwhelmed by the realization that God is "an antinomy—a totality of inner opposites," and as such a victim of the unresolved conflictual forces of divine life itself.[191] Put succinctly, Job realizes that such a God "is too unconscious to be moral."[192] Not only that, he is also less than enamored with the idea of becoming conscious lest he lose the divine indulgence that goes with such an almighty unconsciousness and attendant irresponsibility. Consistent with this side of his psychology Jung refers to God's "fear of becoming conscious."[193] Yet even in the wake of the moral defeat inflicted on Yahweh by Job's superior insight, which not only held but grew stronger through the suffering of Yaweh's mindless assault, the divine reticence toward incarnate self-consciousness remained. Thus Jung writes, in words reminiscent of Augustine's earlier reservations about a too hasty acceptance of the demands of chastity, "God wants to become man, but not quite."[194]

The new morality endemic to this paradigm shift is that of humanity charged with the task of making conscious in itself the self-contradiction in its creator and then cooperating with that creator in resolving the contradiction. This shift in the perception of the divine-human relation brings us to a brief formulation of the crucial foundational difference between a Jungian and Christian spirituality: *In a Christian spirituality an eternally integrated God shares this integration. In the Jungian tradition a yet to be integrated God seeks to become integrated in humanity.*

In such a perspective the human and divine are so intimately related in their very being that human integration and divine integration cannot be separated even potentially. This leads to significant differences in the mo-

---

189. This is the rhythm of individuation Jung seeks to describe in "Transformation Symbolism in the Mass," *Psychology and Religion,* CW 11, pars. 296ff.
190. "Answer to Job," Prefatory Note, *Psychology and Religion,* CW 11, p. 359.
191. Ibid., pars. 567, 584.
192. Ibid., par. 574.
193. Ibid., par. 595.
194. Ibid., par. 740.

tives which each spirituality attaches to God first in creating and then in becoming incarnate. In Christian orthodoxies God is depicted as creating out of a total self-sufficiency to share his goodness with creatures. The medievals used the principle *bonum diffusivum est,* "the good is diffusive of itself," to describe the overflowing of creation as primordially good from a divinity imagined, as with Bonaventure for instance, as a "fontal plenitude."[195] These formulations present initial creation itself as a grace. As such it remains unforced by any serious divine need.

With Jung this vision of creation is not tenable. The creator of human consciousness creates it so that, with the creator's help and with the cooperation of the individual, God can become conscious in human consciousness. Jung thus makes humanity the fourth person in God's own life-process, that dimension in which God and humanity become conscious of each other in processes of mutual maturation and redemption.

At the heart of this partnership is the theme that God's self-contradiction escapes its divine origin and now is humanity's problem as well. This would make for a more realistic version of the Catholic conception of the *analogia entis*, the analogy or likeness between divine and human being. In its Jungian revisioning, the basis of this analogy would be the reflection of the divine contradiction in all that is, and especially in human consciousness where alone the contradiction can be perceptively suffered and hopefully resolved. The more overriding morphology of this mutual redemption is that of humanity's resolution of the divine self-contradiction, both at divinity's insistence and with divinity's help.

This altered view of creation and its necessity flows over into Jung's psycho-theology of incarnation. Traditionally where theologians reflect on the motives of the Incarnation, they see it sometimes as a second divine initiative in gratuitous response to the primordial disaster of Eden. This is the case with Aquinas and most of the Reform tradition. Occasionally, however, the motive of the Incarnation is pictured as providing a certain capstone to creation, bringing creative processes to a culmination in the figure of Christ. This was the case with Scotus and others in the Franciscan tradition. With Jung the motive of the Incarnation is quite different: "To sum up: the immediate cause of the Incarnation lies in Job's elevation, and its purpose is the differentiation of Yaweh's consciousness."[196]

---

195. See Dourley, *Paul Tillich and Bonaventure*, pp. 121ff.
196. "Answer to Job," *Psychology and Religion,* CW 12, par. 642.

Within this perspective the Incarnation becomes as necessary for God as initial creation and is basically a symbol of divinity's continued maturation in human consciousness. For Jung the base meaning of incarnation describes that psychic process in which God becomes progressively conscious through the repeated rhythm of consciousness moving into its divine precedent and returning from it with an ever extended empathy for the totality. As such the Incarnation symbolizes the redemption of both God and humanity in one organic process in which both have been implicated from the outset. In this sense the direction of the evolution of consciousness is toward humanity's conscious appropriation of its native divinity in the experience of the unification of the divine opposites in itself and of the wholeness that attaches to such resolution.

Jung describes this evolution of consciousness when he writes:

> It was only quite late that we realized (or rather, are beginning to realize) that God is Reality itself and therefore—last but not least—man. This realization is a millennial process.[197]

Here Jung is obviously describing this process as currently and slowly working its way into human consciousness. Its radical religious implication of the intimacy and real mutual neediness of the divine and the human was one that White and Buber could not accept.

But Jung's assertion that the development of human consciousness is one in which it redeems or recovers its natural divinity and attendant wholeness is not airy speculation. His psychology is capable of pointing to how and in what areas of life God seeks to become conscious. It does this by placing such value on the legitimate pain suffered by individual or epoch and by fostering the compensation proffered to that pain by the unconscious, whose purpose in history is the wholeness of individual and society. Thus authentic archetypal suffering is humanity's participation in divinity's self-contradiction, and its compensation is divinity's only real presence to humanity. When this pain becomes a form of false suffering inflicted on individual and society by a myth that can no longer serve the interests of wholeness, then compensation offered to consciousness by the unconscious can bear a relieving and whole-making myth which takes on the functioning status of a new revelation. That Jung thought that the unconscious was indeed working such a new revelation is made explicit in

---

197. Ibid., par. 631.

the previously cited conclusion to one of his letters with Victor White: "Christ is still the valid symbol. Only God can 'invalidate' him through the Paraclete."[198]

Consideration of unconscious compensation as the potential bearer of a new revelation touching both individual and society brings us to the last point of tension between a Jungian and Christian spirituality. It is a tension at the core of Jung's proposal that the presiding symbol in the Christian myth, that of the Trinity, cede to that of the quaternity.

The shift to a quaternitarian paradigm is unquestionably the most substantial contribution Jung made to the effort to relate religion and theology to psychology, that is, to relate the experience of the divine to psychic experience. Jung was driven to this position by what we have already seen. The unconscious creates consciousness and is itself the source of all opposites that consciousness perceives. Thus all opposites experienced in creation must exist in their source. But in a Trinitarian God, imaged as God the creator, there is no reference to matter, the body or instinct understood as the opposite of Spirit. There is no reference to evil as the opposite of good. There is no reference to the feminine, the opposite of the masculine.[199] For Jung these missing parts of deity as creator must be restored to deity and deified in creation if God is truly to claim to be the creator of all that is and if the creature is ever again to affirm the sacredness of all that is as an expression of God, the source of the sacred.

However, the process of extending one's sense of what is sacred and, with it, one's sense of what is included in the reality of God as the source of the sacred is, for Jung, not a purely rational exercise. Rather what Jung is saying is that a more life-giving spirituality and its supporting myth must be surfaced, not in an easy jettisoning of the presiding myth, but through the suffering of its one-sidedness. This is the only legitimate condition of ushering into consciousness what will transcend it in cooperation with the whole-making intent of the unconscious and the Self. The recovery of such a myth and its spirituality would compensate what Christianity has

---

198. See above, note 89.
199. Jung makes these points in "A Psychological Approach to the Dogma of the Trinity," *Psychology and Religion*, CW 11, section 5, "The Problem of the Fourth," pars. 243ff. In the face of frequent misrepresentation of Jung on this issue, especially by some feminists, it should here be clearly noted that for Jung the only commonality shared by the body, evil and the feminine is their joint exclusion from Christianity's presiding symbol, the Trinity.

one-sidedly and thus pathologically deified in Spirit, the good and the masculine. The moral demand implicit in the current redemption of God is the birth of a myth and accompanying spirituality which can affirm the sacredness of what is now excluded from the realm of the holy. This would mean a myth in which the holiness of matter is affirmed in union with the world of the Spirit, in which male and female consciously realize a wholesome androgyny, and in which Christ and Satan, two brothers of the same Father, embrace without reserve.[200]

But again the question is, how does one access the energies which now urge such a myth and in the end create it? Jung's answer would be through the discovery of the meaning of the suffering in one's personal life, revealed through a direct dialogue with the God within, the author of all revelation but more importantly and immediately of the revelation tailored to the individual in the form of the nightly dream. Through one's personal response to this inner dialogue the individual becomes the recipient of a private revelation. It is from this process of living into one's own emerging myth that one makes the most significant contribution to the transformation of society. What is involved in this dialogue between the human, suffering some side of the divine contradiction, and the God who suffers toward self-consciousness in human suffering, becomes clearer when one reflects on what Jung meant by the world of the Spirit and so what he might mean by a spirituality grounded in a dialogue with the Spirit.

In a thorough reading of Jung there are at least three major meanings of the term Spirit. He uses it occasionally with the meaning it has in the phrase, "the Spirit Mercurius." Here he simply identifies Mercurius as one Spirit among many. The reality of Mercurius is thus understood as one archetypal power among many. In this sense one could speak of the Spirit of Dionysus, or of Athena or of any other God or Goddess. In a more modern sense Jung's use of the term would coincide with the title of the Fellini movie, *Juliet of the Spirits,* which conveys the idea that autonomous powers invaded and controlled Juliet's life for her weal or woe.

This use of Spirit is modern because it reflects that growing contemporary awareness, to which Jung's psychology has made so significant a contribution, that contact with the archetypal powers of the psyche is the basis of conversation with the Gods, Goddesses and Spirits of the Spirit world. It is to this conversation Jung refers when he writes, "The world of

---

200. See above, note 94.

gods and spirits is truly 'nothing but' the collective unconscious inside me."[201] The phrase "nothing but" is hardly meant to discredit the power of the Spirits. Since as dwellers of the unconscious they are so near to consciousness, precisely the opposite is his intent.

The nearness of the Spirits to consciousness is the basis of a now dawning realization of how seriously the psyche must be taken as the birthplace of divinity which can destroy or enhance humanity. Consciously dialoguing with the Spirit world becomes the basis of a new and demanding morality where the greatest sin is to remain unaware of the unconscious and the overwhelming power of the Spirit world. However, many passages in Jung's work lead the reader to wonder if Jung felt modernity and even its spiritual leaders were up to the rigors of conversations with the Gods. He writes, for instance, "Man's worst sin is unconsciousness, but it is indulged in with the greatest piety even by those who should serve mankind as teachers and examples."[202] He concludes this passage with a plea to the world's leaders to avoid the temptations to unconsciousness held out to them by the certitudes of their own faiths:

> Christianity has shown us the way, but, as the facts bear witness, it has not penetrated deeply enough below the surface. What depths of despair are still needed to open the eyes of the world's responsible leaders, so that at least they can refrain from leading themselves into temptation?[203]

This advance in modern consciousness and morality means that what was projected onto Mount Parnasus in Greek mythology, and even higher in the skies by monotheistic transcendentalism, has, in our epoch, been located in its origins in the deepest dimension of the psyche. In this context Jung refers to what he calls his "demonstration of the psychic origin of religious phenomena."[204] Jung's relocation of the origin of humanity's sense of the divine means further that the analytic hour, where the dream is seen as an individualized revelation, is a conversation with the Gods and Goddesses speaking in the here and now and attempting to find a fuller incarnation in that individual's humanity. Since the deities both author and appear in the dream, this obviously makes the dream and its conscious ap-

---

201. "Commentary on 'The Tibetan Book of the Dead,' " ibid., par. 857.
202. "The Phenomenology of the Spirit in Fairytales," *The Archetypes and the Collective Unconscious,* CW 9i, par. 455.
203. Ibid.
204. "Introduction to the Religious and Psychological Problems of Alchemy," *Psychology and Alchemy,* CW 12, par. 9.

propriation in the analytic hour a sacred event. Analysts must then be excused if they are less than overwhelmed by institutional proclamations of divine appearance and favor when they stare at and listen to the Gods and Goddesses speaking through their clients hour after hour and week after week.

The second sense of Spirit in Jung's work is that of one opposite in a polarity whose other extreme can be described variously as body, matter or instinct.[205] Spirit is here opposed to all that heaviness with its potentially addictive or imprisoning weight which wars against Spirit even to the point of extinguishing it. In this sense Jung understands Christianity and its sister religion, Mithraism, as spiritual religions whose birth occurred as collective compensation to the pervasive excesses committed against the Spirit in the cultures into which these religions were born.[206] In recovering the Spirit from its threatened immersion in all that could devour it, Christianity became the basis of Western culture. Jung describes the Christ figure as our still reigning culture hero, that hero which every culture needs as the cohesive principle around which it builds its cosmology and value system.[207] In this sense we still live with a "spiritual" religion whose one-sided spirituality is problematic.

As seen above in chapter two, Jung suggests in his alchemical work that the processes of spiritualization so valuable in the birth and history of Christianity are only the first stages in the process of a greater wholeness. Jung pays tribute to Christian restraint and asceticism as a necessary preliminary in freeing the soul from an imprisonment in the body which could deny to the soul its own life, dignity and freedom. But once the soul is freed, it must not, for Jung and for the alchemical tradition on which he is here dependent, step through the "window of eternity"[208] and be lost forever to the finite world of human endeavor where alone God can be redeemed and an incarnate and fully authentic spirituality realized.

Rather, the soul freed from the body must return purified into the body.

---

205. See, as typical, Jung's description of the relation of Spirit and instinct in "On the Nature of the Psyche," *The Structure and Dynamics of the Psyche,* CW 8, par. 379: "Spirit and instinct are by nature autonomous and both limit in equal measure the applied field of the will."
206. See *Symbols of Transformation*, CW 5, pars. 102-104.
207. See *Aion*, CW 9ii, par. 69.
208. *Mysterium Coniunctionis*, CW 14, pars. 670, 763. Jung attributes this expression to Leibniz in the first citation.

Jung relates this experience to the *corpus glorificationis*,[209] the glorified body which bears one's eternal truth in time and space. Like the alchemists he calls this state of consciousness a *caelum*,[210] a heaven, and suggests that this experience is truly one of resurrection. In Jung's appropriation of the alchemical tradition it thus becomes obvious that the experience of resurrection is to happen, at least in approximation, within the confines of finitude as the natural culmination of psychological maturation. An old safety slogan read, "Accident is only a word until you have one." In terms of the experiential appropriation of religious symbolism, Jung might well write in the same spirit, "Resurrection is only a word till you have one," and suggest that this event has little to do with physiological death and the return to physical life.

Thus the sense of the *unus mundus* or one world, the culmination of alchemical transformation, describes a wholeness in which the multiplicity of powers in individual life become integrated in the service of that life, even as the individual moves toward an empathic embrace of the totality. In this movement toward unity, all opposites must be included. From this final synthesis nothing that is can be absent without failure of the whole process. Focusing on Spirit as opposite of the embodied, Jung's psychology implies strongly that a one-sided emphasis on Spirit is now a major pathologizing feature in Western culture and that the wider spirit of his psychology seeks a reunion of Spirit with the much maligned body. Such a Spirit would no doubt be of deeper hue and greater heat than the white dove and fire which symbolize the Christian Spirit.

This idea of Spirit as one instance of one opposite now seeking unity with its contradiction at the insistence of the Self, brings us then to the third and most encompassing meaning of Spirit in Jung's work. Here it can be taken as the Spirit of the Self, acting as *spiritus rector*,[211] which both demands and is the result of the unity of all opposites. As such, its realization is the goal of psychological maturation, the process Jung calls individuation. Thus he can write that the movement toward the Self is a movement toward Spirit, not as toward one pole in a polarity but toward that Spirit which integrates and balances all opposites in the life of the indi-

---

209. Ibid., par. 763.
210. Ibid.
211. See "The Alchemical Interpretation of the Fish," *Aion*, CW 9ii, par. 257, and "On the Nature of the Psyche," *The Structure and Dynamics of the Psyche*, CW 8, par. 406.

vidual, even as it relates the individual thus blessed to all that is.

As an example of what Jung means by this, there exists a lengthy passage in which he likens the archetypal unconscious to the color spectrum.[212] At the extremes are the infrared of the instincts and the blue of pure Spirit. Both are pathologizing extremes. In the middle is the ultraviolet, the union of red and blue, latent in the archetypal world, to be differentiated in consciousness and reunited by the Spirit of the Self in a conscious "apocatastasis" from which no opposite is to be excluded.[213] Thus the most foundational meaning of Spirit in Jung's use of the term is the power which works the unity of all opposites and becomes real only as this unity becomes conscious. In this sense, and, in this sense alone, does Jung affirm that the movement to Spirit is the deepest, and, in the end, only movement of the psyche. Jung means this when he writes:

> Psychologically, however, the archetype as an image of instinct is a spiritual goal toward which the whole nature of man strives; it is the sea to which all rivers wend their way, the prize which the hero wrests from the fight with the dragon.[214]

Jung's conception of the movement toward psychological wholeness culminating in a spirituality in which all opposites are united has significant consequences. As stated above, the deepest basis of the tension between Christian spirituality and Jung's psychology is his conviction that the experience of God and the energies that attach to it are endemic to the psyche. But when Spirit as a unity of opposites is related to the Holy Spirit, an even deeper gulf widens between the two. For the Christian Holy Spirit unites the opposites of Father and Son, with all the nuances tradition gives these opposites. Further, the Holy Spirit works to unite the Christian with the unity it works in Trinitarian life. But the Holy or, perhaps unholy, Spirit at work in Jung's understanding of the psyche seeks to include in both divine and human life those dimensions of human experience excluded from the unities worked by the Spirit in the Christian Trinity. Indeed, Jung's Spirit would seek to restore to divine and human life those sides of human experience so often held in contempt by the Christian.

Thus Jung is arguing that the Spirit now at work in a newly emerging spirituality is one which must include what the Christian Spirit was forced

---

212. Ibid., par. 414.
213. Ibid., par. 416.
214. Ibid., par. 415.

to exclude for historical reasons. In giving content to what was excluded he focuses on the feminine, on the reality of the material—the bodily and 'the instinctual—and on the demonic. None of these are included in the Christian deity. Jung affirms that Christian culture now suffers from their exclusion or repression in both personal and social life. The wholeness that the Spirit, in Jung's sense the *spiritus rector* of the Self, now seeks to recover is one in which these realities can once again find divine validation and so return to the human the energies which attach to their divinity.

At times Jung casts this new spirituality in the image of the rerooting of the modern soul in its native divinity. He describes the contemporary rootlessness of a one-sidedly intellectual culture in terms at once poetic and metaphysical:

> But consciousness, continually in danger of being lead astray by its own light of becoming a rootless will o' the wisp, longs for the healing power of nature, for the deep wells of being and for unconscious communion with life in all its countless forms.[215]

Such a rerooting would entail the befriending of the dark and excluded shadow and marriage with the interior contrasexual, which reestablishes commerce with the origin and renewer of consciousness, that sea of creativity which mythology as humanity's first psychology knows as the Great Goddess or Mother. This Mother can appreciate her monotheistic, wholly conscious and transcendent male Gods. Indeed she can smile on her offspring, the divine fathers, sons and messiahs, and their devotional constituencies, since she is the mother of them all.

However, a careful reading of Jung and a more thorough assimilation of his understanding of the Spirit currently moving through humanity shows the power of the Goddess working to corrode such transcendent, largely male, Gods in favor of a more immediate interior conversation with her more expansive empathies. Our collective survival may hinge on her ability to dissolve these transcendent Gods and their divisive earthly communities by offering to them a more accepting and inclusive embrace of the totality she constantly sponsors. But if her empathies are more extensive than the patriarchies that owe their existence to her—even as they deny her—such extended empathy becomes most real only in direct conversation with her and her archetypal powers. This was the substance of the al-

---

215. *Symbols of Transformation*, CW 5, par. 299.

chemical *opus*, and according to Jung it is the work of each individual life-time toward the incarnation of the Self in individual and collective reality.

Perhaps Jung's greatest contribution to the making of a workable modern myth with a greater survival potential than Christianity lies in his insistence on the importance of establishing this conversation with the divine matrix of all consciousness.

5

Accessing the Spirits:
Jung and the Shamanic

To this point in the discussion, considerable attention has been given to
Jung's psychology as promoting an unmediated dialogue with the world of
the Spirits within the psyche. The dream remained Jung's preferred access
to the spiritual world. But two other major avenues to the Spirit world
which fascinated Jung were the shamanic and the mystical.

The link between aboriginal experience and that of certain canonized
doctors of the Church might seem obscure. However, from Jung's perspective, the bond between shaman and mystic lay in their immediate,
sometimes repeated and always intense experience of the world of the
Spirits. Because the sometimes cultured mystic and the primordial human
shared the same experience, Jung again suggests that humanity universally
both seeks the energies of the Spirits and is perennially vulnerable to their
invasion. Thus an examination of Jung's understanding of the shaman's
and the mystic's access to the deeper energies of the psyche is in direct
continuity with the foregoing discussion of interiority as the source of the
human experience of divinity.

Jung's interest in shamanism is much in evidence throughout his writings, and seems to be enjoying something of a renewal in the work of
those who continue to develop his psychology.[216] Among many scattered
references in Jung's *Collected Works* there are two essays particularly
pertinent to the shamanic reality.[217] More recent statements on Jung and
shamanism contend that Jung could appreciate shamans because he was
one. The suggestion is that he had undergone shamanic-like experiences,
especially of initiation, at key points in his life, most intensely in the wake

---

216. See, for instance, *The Shaman From Elko* (San Francisco: C.G. Jung Institute
of San Francisco, (1978); also Thomas Belmonte, "The Trickster and the Sacred
Clown: Revealing the Logic of the Unspeakable," and Stanley Diamond, "Jung
Contra Freud: What It Means To Be Funny," in *C.G. Jung and the Humanities*:
Toward a Hermeneutics of Culture, eds. Karin Barnaby and Pellegrino D'Acierno
(Princeton: Princeton University Press, 1990), pp. 45-75.
217. "On The Psychology of the Trickster Figure," *The Archetypes and the Collec-
tive Unconscious,* CW 9i, and "Archaic Man," *Civilization in Transition,* CW 10.

of his painful break with Freud.[218] These personal experiences then enabled him to depict the maturational process at the heart of his psychology in a shamanic paradigm.[219]

Thus understood, the analytic process can easily be depicted as a conversation with the Spirit world and so as a shamanic event. This understanding of therapy as shamanism or vice versa was a motivational force in Jung's life-long interest in anthropology. The guiding premise was that primordial or aboriginal imagery could appear in the dream material of the "enlightened" but uprooted modern, material which comes from the same world in which the shaman is so much at home and which lives for the shaman with a vitality denied to the more pallid consciousness of contemporary Western culture.

Jung's references to shamanism include his essay on the trickster, of whom he writes: "His universality is co-extensive, so to speak, with that of shamanism, to which, as we know, the whole phenomenology of spiritualism belongs."[220] In these words Jung closely associates the trickster with the shaman and understands both as having immediate access to the world of the Spirits. For Jung the Spirits, as distinct from souls as personal, are "complexes of the collective unconscious."[221] As such, the Spirits are transpersonal forces to which the ego can relate but never fully assimilate, let alone manipulate, through rational or willful coercion. Rather the guiding Spirit of the Self orchestrates the dialogue between the ego and the Spirit world in a maturing psyche. The Spirits thus understood are the bearers to consciousness of the numinous energies of the archetypal powers of the unconscious.

The questions arise then, "What archetypal energies or depths are engaged by the shaman in entering the world of the Spirits?" In his work on the trickster, Jung suggests that the shaman returns to that primordial level of the psyche analogous to the Christian depiction of the garden of Eden in which all forms of life—divine, animal and human—were not yet severed

218. C. Groesbeck, "C.G. Jung and the Shaman's Vision," *Journal of Analytical Psychology*, vol. 34, no. 3 (July 1989), pp. 255-275. See also Jung's documentation of his shamanic experience in *Memories, Dreams, Reflections*, p. 170.
219. J.V. Downton, "Individuation and Shamanism," *Journal of Analytical Psychology*, vol 34, no. 1 (January 1989), pp. 73-88.
220. "On the Psychology of the Trickster Figure," *The Archetypes and the Collective Unconscious,* CW 9i, par. 457.
221. "The Psychological Foundations of Belief in Spirits," *The Structure and Dynamics of the Psyche,* CW 8, par. 597.

from or in conflict with each other.[222] In doing this the shaman engages the archetypal world in a manner not easily reducible to one or other archetypal depiction. For in one and the same experience the shaman takes humanity back to its collective shadow in the form of the animal from which all humanity derives; but this "therapeutic anamnesis"[223] or recall also reminds humanity of the divinity of its animality. In working this reconnection with its lowly yet divine origin, the shaman brings back to consciousness the energies of a humanity at one with nature.

For Jung this sense of totality is painfully absent to contemporary consciousness and culture. Modern shamanic consciousness, itself in touch with these unities and so capable of mediating them to others, would thus be both awkward and vulnerable but, like the trickster's, the bearer of the individual and collective future. In this context Jung suggests that the modern shaman, like the shaman of old, also becomes something of a redeemer of society by first contacting and then mediating to it the Spirits which "seek to replace an inadequate attitude of a whole people by a new one."[224] In a culture pathologized by an appreciation of the disembodied Spirit and intellect, with an accompanying contempt for the animal and instinctual, Jung strongly intimates that the healing role of the shaman may be as urgent now as it was in the past.

In the role of societal renewal and reinvigoration, the shamanic tradition is perhaps one of the earliest expressions of the fundamental task of historical humanity, namely the humanization and education of God through human consciousness. In his essay on the trickster Jung refers to the shaman as someone who, like Job, experiences the overpowering rage of Yahweh in the interests of Yaweh's becoming conscious and so humanized.[225] Thus the shaman, like Job, has experienced the overwhelming power of divinity and, in withstanding it, leads his society into a more adequate and human relation to it. Moreover, this experience points to the presence of good and evil Spirits which when faced in oneself are deprived

---

222. "On the Psychology of the Trickster Figure," *The Archetypes and the Collective Unconscious,* CW 9i, par. 472: "He is a forerunner of the saviour, and, like him, God, man, and animal at once."

223. Ibid., par. 474.

224. "The Psychological Foundations of Belief in Spirits," *The Structure and Dynamics of the Psyche,* CW 8, par. 597.

225. "On the Psychology of the Trickster Figure," *The Archetypes and the Collective Unconscious,* CW 9i, par. 458. This theme is the substance of Jung's late work, "Answer to Job," *Psychology and Religion,* CW 11.

of their capacity to be projected onto another. In a final note in this essay, aimed at the modern situation, Jung notes that such awareness of the spirits and so of the collective shadow is the first step in preventing its projection onto competing collectivities.[226] Thus an awareness of common origins and of the universality of the Spirits breeds a socially safer—because more encompassing—empathy for what is human in all its often contradictory archetypal expressions.[227]

In his essay on archaic man, Jung's thrust is somewhat different. He repeats his theme that, though we may today be possessed of more sophisticated "mental equipment," our consciousness is, nevertheless, as psychically continuous with its archaic origins as is the body with its mammalian ancestors.[228] But he goes on to distinguish between Western and primordial consciousness under the rubric that neither is in and of itself superior but distinguished by different "presuppositions."[229] The difference centers around the Western predilection for reason, scientific law and an exclusive reliance on the principle of causality turned to the domination of nature wholly divested of any numinous aura.[230] The shadow side of this consciousness is its abhorrence of the prerational and irrational. It is baffled in the face of chance which when dramatically negative plunges it into archaic, and often religious, responses which belie its shallow absorption in the world of reason, causality and statistics.[231]

The archaic mind, in contrast, denies the possibility of chance. It assumes that every event is an expression of willful intent of an arbitrary, superior power.[232] Jung attributes this sense of a presiding power external to the psyche to the fact that the primordial mind is given more to projection than is the contemporary Western mind, where projection is largely confined to the religious sphere considered as a segment of life discontinuous from the allegedly "secular."[233] The positive side of this conscious-

---

226. "On the Psychology of the Trickster Figure," *The Archetypes and the Collective Unconscious,* CW 9i, par. 484.
227. Ibid., par. 485. Jung's argument here is that making the collective shadow conscious enhances the collective anima as the basis of a wider empathy in intercollective relationships.
228. "Archaic Man," *Civilization in Transition,* CW 10, pars. 104-105.
229. Ibid., par. 107.
230. Ibid., pars. 135-136.
231. Ibid., par. 123.
232. Ibid., pars. 117-118.
233. Ibid., par. 132.

ness is the primitive's openness to a sense of the ultimacy and meaning of everyday events. This openness is not found in the so-called sophisticated consciousness of the West, religiously and culturally impoverished by its imprisonment in the world of reason.

The questionable side of archaic consciousness is that it lives under the tyranny of the deities these projections create, as if they had an existence independent of the psyche that creates them.[234] This pathology would be in evidence even in the West in the case of Jung's father's loss of energy to a God created by the psyche beyond the psyche, a God to whom his father sacrificed so much of his humanity. And yet Jung is here presenting the West with a difficult if not insoluble problem. For the deepest impulse of Jung's psychology is to unite opposites. Such an impulse is driven then toward the resolving synthesis of Western uprooted consciousness and that of the aboriginal mind, both valid aspects of a total humanity. His psychology seriously asks if such a synthesis is possible and if so, how? Ideally the synthesis to the problem he here poses would take the form of a consciousness which would retain its intellectual and technological acuity, while honoring the archetypal powers of the psyche. The question remains as to whether this consciousness is possible and what it would look like, since obviously it does not yet exist as a phenomenological reality.

Nevertheless, Jung's understanding of the psyche does insist that only the conscious recovery of these primal energies would revitalize Western culture and at the same time divest Western consciousness of its aggressiveness in the service of death. Further, his psychology suggests strongly that where the primordial energies of the psyche cannot be surfaced, let alone honored, in institutional religions under their servitude to divinities in projection, religion will increasingly and consciously recover its original gnostic-shamanic impulse in the form of the individual's immediate dialogue with the daemon, divine and demonic, within. Jung believes that this way of accessing the world of Spirits is the program the unconscious currently sponsors in the evolution of human consciousness. He writes, "Everything of a divine or daemonic character outside us must return to the psyche, the inside of the unknown man, whence it apparently originated."[235] Shamans might lack the resources to so describe what they do, but Jung may describe their journey rather well as primarily interior and,

---

234. Ibid., par. 138.
235. "Psychology and Religion," *Psychology and Religion,* CW 11, par. 141.

on this basis, recommend it to the religiously deprived Westerner.

In his essay on archaic man, Jung analyzes the psychogenesis of *mana*[236] and, elsewhere in his work, its functional equivalents in a variety of cultures.[237] He concludes that the attribution of *mana* to the shaman or holy person is really an externalization of the sacred powers that exist in everyone. He writes, " 'Fetching God from without' is the equivalent of the primitive view that *tondi* can be got from outside."[238] It has been pointed out that the phrase "fetching God from outside" was borrowed from Eckhart. It is an expression of Eckhart's understanding that God is accessed from within. In Jung's usage of the phrase, he intends it to mean that God is not fetched from without either as beyond the psyche in projection or through the mediation of shaman or priest. To relate to such a God or to those institutionally designated or empowered to fetch God, is for Jung a failure to realize that God is within and that every individual is a priest or shaman when the divine impulse arising from the psyche is consciously engaged.

Reimagining mediation in shamanic terms would not deny the value of the shaman's role in extending to others the healing effects of his or her personal experience. In "Archaic Man," Jung leaves unanswered the question of the shaman being a peculiarly appropriate object of his community's projection, a hook for its vesting him with an alleged familiarity with the Spirits. Indeed, the shaman's personal openness to the world of the Spirits, sometimes coupled with a painful initiation into it, may give to the shaman a peculiar aptness to mediate such experience to others. Jung seems to recognize this "objective" side in the projection which creates the holy man or woman when he argues that the shaman, as a "gifted individual," makes available to all, through ritual reenactment, the healing experience of inner divinity surfaced from the shaman's personal journey into the depths of the universal psyche.[239]

Thus, read in the total context of his remarks, Jung is arguing that the sacred and healing powers projected onto the shaman, which admittedly the shaman has intensely and immediately experienced, are humanity's

---

236. "Archaic Man," *Civilization in Transition,* CW 10, par. 128.
237. "On Psychic Energy," *The Structure and Dynamics of the Psyche,* CW 8, pars. 124-125.
238. *Psychological Types,* CW 6, par. 417.
239. "Transformation Symbolism in the Mass," *Psychology and Religion,* CW 11, par. 448.

universal possession. By implication, if the projection of healing divinity onto the shaman were withdrawn, this could lead the individual to a conscious realization of the universality of the shaman's experience of the Spirit world and the discovery of its potentially healing and whole-making powers in oneself.

In Jung's understanding, this process of the universal recovery of one's shamanic nature would be closely akin to what happened in the later Egyptian period in the universalization of the pharaoh's divine ancestry through its extension to everyone in the kingdom. It would also be akin to Jung's extension of the reality of Christ as both divine and human to every human, as a symbolic description of the divine nature of the Self which becomes incarnate in everyone in natural processes of individuation.[240]

To any and every tradition based on any kind of sacred hierarchy or priesthood understood to mediate participation in the divine, grace or redemptive transformation, Jung's psychology would respond that every individual is a priest and has immediate access to redemption through the psyche. In terms of whatever may be meant by salvation, Jung's analysis of the shamanic forces the conclusion that there is nothing that the priest can do for one that one cannot do for oneself.

This view would not necessarily eliminate the function of priest or dramaturge. But it would ask those filling that role to become conscious of what they are about. It would demand of anyone exercising a formal priestly function the realization that the priesthood and the sacramental reality work to make conscious what are universal latencies in the human psyche. Like the shaman, the priest may be peculiarly gifted in terms of a sense of the sacred and may be formally vested with societal recognition. But Jung would insist that the personal gift of a sensitivity for the sacred which warrants societal approbation belongs to the universal psyche itself. Other views of priesthood and sacramentality relating the ministerial function to the mediation of a redemption not already latent and demanded by the human psyche would quickly degenerate into a literal and magical manipulation of the world of the Spirit. They would also offend the dignity of priest and community by plunging both into a profound unconsciousness

---

240. See "A Psychological Approach to the Dogma of the Trinity," ibid., par. 289. Here Jung describes the universal "divinizing" power of the Self in these terms: "Through the descent of the Holy Ghost, the self of man enters into a relationship of unity with the substance of God." In the context Jung extends the *homoousia* of Christ to humanity as such.

of what happens in the effective religious event.

In Jung's analysis, the projection, and thus alienation, of one's own sacred power in fact creates this power in the shaman. The implications of this are far-reaching. Much the same kind of projecting goes on in the creation of contemporary religious figures, vesting them with immense power. The most obvious of these offices and figures is the papacy. The cult of the pope originated in the nineteenth century when Pius IX had himself declared infallible at Vatican I in 1870 in the face of considerable opposition. Many of the council fathers walked out rather than consent to the doctrine.[241] All but the bishop of Little Rock, Arkansas, eventually were persuaded to consent. Even on the occasion of its proposal in the nineteenth century the cult of the papacy was seen through by such loyal Catholics as the German-British historian, Lord Acton. He wrote of his opposition to it in these now famous terms:

> Power tends to corrupt, and absolute power corrupts absolutely. Great men are almost always bad men. . . . There is no worse heresy than that the office sanctifies the holder of it.[242]

Lord Acton was not working with Jungian conceptions of projection. With them he could well have argued that the withdrawal of the projection of such power from the papacy would relocate the power in the community and ultimately in the individual, perhaps accompanied by the conscious recognition that the power was initially projected onto the papacy out of an unconscious but understandable need for human certitude. In this matter again, Jung's views are hardly divested of political and social consequence. Should the popes in their current self-understanding be seen through as vested with a religious *mana* not unlike that of the shaman, the recovery of the projection which creates them would bring down the first modern and currently still powerful multinational corporation. The present pope cultivates the projection and successfully engages the media in it by the promulgation of Vatican policies hostile to the spirit of Vatican II through papal journeys and circuses staged throughout the world. The recovery of the projection that funds such unconsciousness in both the holder of the office and those fascinated with it would work a reform of

---

241. See H.A. MacDougall, *Lord Acton on Papal Power* (London: Sheed and Ward, 1973), p. 14.
242. Letter to Bishop Creighton, 1887, in *The Liberal Tradition*, eds. A. Bullock and M. Schock (Oxford: Clarendon Press, 1967), p. 124.

the papacy far more radical and much more lasting than that attempted at Vatican II, where efforts to contain papal power through collegial sharing were easily defeated by the Vatican when the Council disbanded.

In a wry conclusion to his essay on archaic consciousness, Jung points out that the primitive idea of an arbitrary invading deity is by no means foreign to the West where the scientific mind prevails—except on Sunday when it bows to the intervention of supernatural, divine powers.[243] He writes of this strange Western regression: "Religious thought keeps alive the archaic state of mind even today, in a time bereft of gods. Untold millions of people still think like this."[244] Jung's words are still pertinent. The imagination need not be stretched to envision the most committed military scientist or strategist burning candles before a preferred deity for divine protection of a son sent to the Gulf War.

At the end of this piece, with the waffling that so often characterizes his thought on these issues, Jung asks if the primitive mind and its relation to disconnected and transcendent Spirits may be correct. Somewhat whimsically he refuses to rule on the issue. However, when his works are read organically Jung leaves little doubt that the experience of the Spirit world is that of the impact of intrapsychic archetypal powers on consciousness. Now that this is known, he pleads with the West not to dismiss the power for good or evil of the Spirits because their psychic origin is unveiled but, on the contrary, to seize the new understanding as the occasion for entering a conscious dialogue with the Spirits as a most powerful strategy to combat collective possession by them.[245]

Three themes, in particular, in Jung's appropriation of shamanism illustrate how shamanic phenomena illuminate the process of individuation, understood as an ongoing, cyclic entrance into the world of the unconscious and return from it, enhanced by an unmediated encounter with the Spirits. These are the shamanic usages of imagery and rituals centering on stones or crystals, on trees, and on dismemberment or sacrifice.

Jung was aware of the flint-man tradition in a number of Amerindian traditions.[246] In many of these, the bringer of culture is understood to be made of flint and in some variations the stone man is also a bearer of light

243. "Archaic Man," *Civilization in Transition,* CW 10, par. 143.
244. Ibid., par. 138.
245. "The Phenomenology of the Spirit in Fairytales," *The Archetypes and the Collective Unconscious,* CW 9i, par. 455.
246. *Alchemical Studies*, CW 13, pars. 132-133.

and occasionally of a liquid light. The stone man is also related to the myth of the virgin birth, a myth Jung understands to point to the birth of the Self into consciousness and so to a universal psychic movement. The religious nature of the flint man is evident in his sometimes being cast as the validating ancestor of the priestly caste. In some shamanic traditions crystals are mediating powers from the crystal throne of a sky God and sometimes the stone man is a fallen star.

For Jung the stone can symbolize the immortality of the Self, that power in which the eternal truth of the individual is grounded, and which seeks ever greater incarnation in the consciousness of the individual as one moves throughout a lifetime toward one's destined "more compendious" or "supraordinate" personality.[247] The stone or crystal as living and luminous so constitutes a powerful symbol of the Self as the immortal ground of individual life. Shamanic imagery would thus imply that the shaman accesses the eternal and unchangeable upon which the human rests and can lead others into this truth in themselves.

One side of Jung's understanding of the truth of the Self is that it has about it the quality of eternity or of the immutable, which sustains the individual in the passage through finitude in such a manner that it precedes, supports and in the end is the goal of such passage. The eternity of the Self is more than suggested in Jung's lines reminiscent of Eckhart's sense of the eternal with which Eckhart felt himself to remain continuous in time: "Just as a man still is what he always was, so he already is what he will become."[248] The same sense of living continuity with an eternal and generative precedent is strongly suggested when Jung writes,

> The self, like the unconscious, is an *a priori* existent out of which the ego evolves. It is, so to speak, an unconscious prefiguration of the ego. It is not I who create myself, rather I happen to myself.[249]

This insight would not be foreign to either shaman or mystic, who apparently have such experiential access to their native eternal being and support in their voyage through time.

From a clinical viewpoint, Jung observed that not a few of his clients who were consciously unaware of shamanic traditions surfaced shamanic

---

247. See "Transformation Symbolism in the Mass," *Psychology and Religion,* CW 11, pars. 390-391.
248. Ibid., par. 390.
249. Ibid., par. 391.

motifs directly from the unconscious in the course of therapy.[250] One such motif was the shamanic tree. It had, for Jung, a wealth of meaning. It symbolized the ascent of the soul upward to its higher truth, often depicted as the anima, sometimes in the form of a snake, who drew the shaman toward his eternal bride or celestial wife,[251] the *ayami*, his familiar protective Spirit and also nourishing mother.[252] In his appreciation of this motif Jung evidences the ambiguity and danger attached to entrance into the world of the heavenly bride or Great Mother. Not to do so is to remain divorced from the energies of the Spirit world, unable to feed or heal oneself or others. But to enter into a permanent bond with one's celestial wife is to lose one's consciousness to her in psychotic removal from the everyday world.[253] Thus the shaman's successful incest with the Great Goddess must be one of entering in and return if the shaman is to mediate the life of the Spirit to the community.

Nor should one conclude from the imagery of the tree that the shaman's journey is one-sidedly spiritual. Though he finds his eternal bride in the top of the tree in a moment that can be at once the possibility of death and yet new life, the tree itself goes into the depths of the earth and so unites sky and ground. The image of the inverted tree implies that the shaman has roots in heaven from whence he derives his "mystical organs,"[254] while the tree as maternal with its roots in the earth also relates the shaman to "the chthonic world and its transitoriness."[255] Thus the shaman must be stretched out, one might say crucified, between earth and sky as he experiences their connection in himself and mediates their integrating and healing power to others.

Here Jung's reflection on the shaman's journey intersects with his understanding of tree and root imagery in alchemy. In this tradition the source of all, the *prima materia*, is the *radix ipsius*, the root of itself,[256] which Jung equates with the *increatum*,[257] the uncreated and the *dea*

---

250. *Alchemical Studies*, CW 13, par. 305.
251. "Concerning the Archetypes," *The Archetypes and the Collective Unconscious,* CW 9i, par. 115, and note 8, where Jung acknowledges his dependence on Mircea Eliade.
252. *Alchemical Studies*, CW 13, par. 460.
253. Ibid., par. 457.
254. Ibid., par. 462.
255. Ibid., par. 457.
256. *Psychology and Alchemy*, CW 12, par. 429.
257. Ibid., par. 430.

mater,[258] the Mother Goddess. Through linking the imagery of these admittedly disparate traditions, Jung would suggest, then, that shaman, alchemist and mystic travel to the divine source of all that is, to the Great Mother herself, and in their return share her health and wealth with their community.

Shamanic suffering introduces the theme of dismemberment and sacrifice. Jung relates this motif in its shamanic form directly to alchemy,[259] and through alchemy to gnosticism and to mystical experience as similar and unmediated experiences of the suffering attendant to significant archetypal transformation. In whatever tradition it appears, Jung identifies the core meaning of dismemberment imagery with psychic death and rebirth.[260] In a shamanic context it would point to the psycho-spiritual death preceding reconstitution and so new life. If the idea of taking on a body of stone or quartz is combined with dismemberment and reconstitution, then the symbolism would point to rebirth into the immortality of the Self.

In thus associating the tortures of the shaman with the alchemical priest Zosimos[261] and, by extension, with the Christ figure, Jung contends that the symbolism of such suffering points to the suffering endemic to the process of individuation itself. In this context he tends to dismiss the idea of vicarious suffering.[262] How could someone suffer to another's maturity? Though shamans and saviors may undergo such suffering on behalf of all, for Jung the suffering remains external and so nontransformative unless it is allowed into one's personal life as the cost of recreation.

Some of Jung's most telling remarks about shamanism occur in his discussion of the archetypal meaning of the Catholic Mass. Here he depicts the individuation process as one in which ego and Self each enact the role of priest and victim. The Self, as priest, demands the death of the ego so that the Self can become increasingly incarnate in its victim in the interests of the deepening and extension of the ego's conscious empathies. But the Self, in allowing itself to become incarnate and finite, is victim to the priestly character of the ego which cooperates with the Self in the alchemical *opus* through which the Self suffers its becoming real in the finitudes

---

258. Ibid., par. 431.
259. *Alchemical Studies*, CW 13, par. 91, note 4.
260. "Transformation Symbolism in the Mass," *Psychology and Alchemy*, CW 11, par. 346, note 9. Here again Jung cites Eliade.
261. See "The Vision of Zosimos," ibid.
262. Ibid., par. 410.

of consciousness. This process for Jung delineates the role of humanity's participation in the creation of God, so that the resultant divine consciousness can be described as the product or son of human endeavor, the alchemical *filius philosophorum*.[263] Needless to say, this implies that God cannot become real, that is, incarnate in human consciousness, without human cooperation. Human cooperation in the creation of God, a foundational point in Jung's appropriation of alchemy, is a theological implication which would stretch the boundaries of most orthodoxies.

Jung sums up much of his understanding of the meaning of images and rites of sacrificial suffering, as developed from their shamanic origins, in these lines:

> The shaman's experience of sickness, torture, death, and regeneration implies, at a higher level, the idea of being made whole through sacrifice, of being changed by transubstantiation and exalted to the pneumatic man—in a word, of apotheosis.[264]

Jung suggests here that transubstantiation does not mean the transformation of subhuman elements into the divine, but the transubstantiation of humanity itself into the divine through the internalization of what the rites, early undergone by the shaman, express externally.

He makes his point even more clearly when he contends that the archetypal meaning of the Catholic Mass had already been prefigured in shamanic consciousness and enactment. He writes,

> The Mass is the summation and quintessence of a development which began many thousands of years ago and with progressive broadening and deepening of consciousness, gradually made the isolated experience of specifically gifted individuals the common property of a larger group.[265]

Among the "gifted individuals" possessed by the archetype of death and rebirth which gradually came to sophisticated ritual consciousness and enactment in the Mass, Jung would certainly and gladly include the shaman.

In conclusion then, one asks what consequences might be drawn from Jung's appreciation of shamanism, especially in the interest of cultivating a more vital and global spirituality. This question is prompted by the extensive, indeed, foundational critique of the spiritual sterility which runs

---

263. Ibid., par. 400.
264. Ibid., par. 448.
265. Ibid.

throughout Jung's psycho-cultural analysis of the modern West.[266] Jung claims that he was forced to enter the world of theology to find out why it could no longer mediate spiritual life to its Christian constituency.[267] In typical formulations he contends that the meaning of dogma and symbol has become a form of "sacrosanct unintelligibility,"[268] and that the meaning of ritual has been lost to the West by a too conscious religiosity working to sever rather than connect consciousness with its rootedness in the divine. In this context Jung's psychology is an apology for the recovery of a gnostic, or alchemical religious consciousness which would work to enable the disconnected Western mind to reexperience without mediation the libidinal energies of its divine ground, first penetrated by the shaman.

These foundational themes in Jung's appreciation of shamanism are not without contemporary value, though current revaluations of shamanistic imagery and practice are clothed in bitter paradox. Jung's appreciation suggests that shamans were among the first to undergo the intense experience of spiritual death and resurrection. As such, shamanism was a spiritual predecessor of the European religion which conquered and largely destroyed the Amerindian culture. The paradox is heightened by Jung's assertion that the Christian liturgy and myth were also based on the rhythm of death and resurrection, even though maimed through their literal and historical expropriation to themselves of so universal a spiritual dynamic. From a Jungian perspective, one might suggest that it was precisely because the myth had been debased to an historical incident, and so divested of deeper and more universal religious import, that the imperial Christian mind could not see the same patterns of transformation at work in the culture they felt compelled to convert to their later variant of the myth in a process now recognized as cultural genocide.

Today some descendants of the perpetrators of the original offense are ready to recognize and apologize for it. In the summer of 1991 the Oblate Conference of Canada, representing 1200 missionary priests, many of whom had worked with Amerindians, offered "an apology for certain aspects of that presence and ministry."[269] The document apologizes for the

---

266. See my *The Illness That We Are*.
267. "A Psychological Approach to the Dogma of the Trinity," *Psychology and Religion*, CW 11, Introduction, pars. 169-171.
268. Ibid., par. 170.
269. *An Apology to the First Nations of Canada by the Oblate Conference of Canada*.

superior attitude of Christian Europe toward the first nations of Canada. It is interesting to note that the document credits the social sciences rather than Christian reflection or theology with identifying such a lethal superior attitude. This fact points both to the higher moral sense often informing the social sciences and to the sad truth that at least the Roman Church lacks the critical perspective and moral resources seriously to reform itself. The apology reads in part,

> Anthropological and sociological insights of the late 20th century have shown how deep, unchallenged, and damaging was the naive cultural, ethnic, linguistic, and religious superiority complex of Christian Europe when its peoples met and interrelated with the aboriginal peoples of North America.[270]

The document does not mention the contribution of psychology to the insights which now condemn such religious imperialism, but surely the Spirit of Jung's psychology would contribute to the current and growing sense of its wrongness. The document goes on to apologize for

> the cultural, ethnic, linguistic, and religious imperialism that was part of the mentality with which the peoples of Europe first met the aboriginal peoples and which consistently has lurked behind the way the Native peoples of Canada have been treated by civil governments and by the churches.[271]

This is a breath of fresh air. It is a frank and candid act of corporate repentance for a wrong committed. Though it represents a relatively small group, it sets a precedent for broader ecclesial repentance, greatly needed but rarely forthcoming. Such a penitent statement could be extended to many other areas of readily imaginable Roman ecclesial guilt, such as depriving women of leadership roles in the church (illegal in Canada and much of the West for any corporation other than the Church), its family and divorce morality, its attitude toward the gay community, its manipulation of male sexuality through nonoptional celibacy in the priesthood in the interest of power and the maintenance of the current order—and the list could go on.

In the current climate the Oblate document is particularly encouraging in the wake of the Vatican's effective defeat of the freer spirit of Vatican II

---

270. Ibid.
271. Ibid.

and in the face of the fact that the Inquisition with its multiple silencings since Vatican II, in the mid-sixties, has been more active than at any time since it squelched Catholic thought early in the twentieth century with its condemnation of Modernism. Thus concerned Roman and Christian circles remain grateful to the courage of those who forged the document. Yet it raises far deeper questions, which few have so far pursued though they follow so obviously from the document itself, questions central to Jung's understanding of the psyche and of the myth it currently seeks to surface. These deeper questions center on the extent of the apology.

It is all very well to apologize for blatantly destructive forms of earlier European and Christian religious imperialism. But how can such imperialism be avoided when it is based on the claim of a final revelation through a definitive intervention of God in an historical person founding an historical church as the official bearer of such revelation? Is not the claim to possess such finality the ultimate form of religious imperialism which underlies the aggressiveness of the missionary endeavor, of religious crusades and wars, and, in the end, the holocaust? How can monotheisms themselves escape the violence that results when any claim to divine favor is made exclusive to one community and these claims are made by more than one community? Can the bloodshed that results when such communities intersect geographically be described as anything other than a systemic necessity of such faiths? What restraint, human or divine, can be placed on the claim that God has exhaustively, or even in a privileged manner, revealed himself historically to a chosen group? How can such a claim result in anything other than a mandate to the chosen to kill or convert?

Thus the apology, confined to a particular time and religious interface, moves immediately to the Christological question. How can claims of Christ's uniqueness as the bringer of a final revelation be anything but imperialistic, with the woeful consequences for which the document apologizes? Are claims to the unique revelation of or in Christ also to be apologized for? Is there any serious format for asking the question, "Is the Good News still Good or where did it go wrong?" From the Christological question the apology forces the missiological question. How can anyone representing Christ as God's final revelation be anything but imperialistic when approaching an integral culture not sharing this view and vested with its own religion? Can anyone who claims to be the exclusive "way, truth and life" be distinguished from the consciousness of a James Bond with a license to kill on behalf of his truth? Should the connection of Jesus and

James Bond, at least as currently encoded in the minds of devotees, be scrutinized in the interests of humanity surviving its religious impulse?

In chapter three we faced these questions from the resources of Jung's psychology. A religious community need not be imperialistic if it were prepared to acknowledge the universal basis of religion in humanity itself, in the collective unconscious. This realization would ground an appreciation of the fact that many religions and their expressions would be needed to manifest the possibly inexhaustible fecundity of that ground. The relativity attaching to the recognition of religion as grounded in the human would foster a sense of appreciation and complementarity between religions rather than fear, hatred and the need to convert. Finally the realization that each individual has unmediated access to the source from which the world religions spring would make of the individual who responds consciously to that source the author of his or her individual myth and so of a consciousness hostile to religious imperialism. Though these values may not satisfy, indeed might corrode, the faith which must assert the superiority of one's God and revelation, they would seem to be the minimal values which will control the future if humanity is to survive.

The discussion of Jung and shamanism should not end without mention of problems which occur in Jung's appropriation of that tradition and by extension in the manner in which it may be currently helpful to the West. The first question is the familiar hermeneutical one. For while Jung appreciates the shamanic experience and tradition, he also proposes a psychological hermeneutic which lays bare its psychodynamics. To many anthropologists this can be offensive because it would seem to be a mechanical imposition of psychological categories on experiences too diverse and ineffable to be so categorized. This objection may be muted by the realization that Jung's basic attitude to shamanism is one of appreciation of its spiritual vitality and depth. In effect he is trying to show its validity and power by relating it so closely to the gnostic, alchemical and mystical traditions as neglected sides of the human resource which humanity now dearly needs to recover. One should thus respect his intent. Rather than force his categories upon it, he is trying to cultivate an appreciation of shamanism by giving it and aboriginal spirituality the place they should hold as human spiritual resources in a culture undergoing spiritual starvation because so long removed from them.

The further question would then arise, "Can one made aware of the psychodynamics of shamanic experience personally reappropriate it?" Or does the very knowledge of what happens to the shaman forbid the recovery of such experience as a living option for revitalizing contemporary spirituality? Jung thought not. Obviously he would have no more respect for a literal reenacting of shamanic rites than he would have for a Christian imitating Christ through growing a beard and wearing sandals. Rather he would see the shaman as someone who entered, lived out of and mediated the vitalities of the unconscious. And this cyclical immersion in the source of the multiple is the spiritual resource which forever validates shamanic endeavor in whatever culture or mode it occurs.

The intensity and immediacy of the nightly dream became for Jung the preferred access to the world of the Spirits to which the shaman had initially journeyed. And since this is a universal propensity it is always there. What is not there is respect for the dream as the voice of God dictating one's personal revelation. Recovered respect for shamanic experience could only lead to recovered respect for this voice and a tendency to listen to it. Thus in the end his appreciation of shamanism does not depotentiate it by exposing its dynamics. The opposite is true. By giving a psychological framework to shamanic experience Jung invites his contemporaries deprived of life's vitalities, often by their religion itself, to reexperience in themselves the shaman's immediate conversation with the Spirits.

Thus Jung would offer to his culture the conscious reappropriation of shamanic experience or its functional equivalent as a major resource for a more intense, sustaining and safer spirituality in the current religious wasteland of the West.

6

Toward an Apophatic Psychology: Jung's Appropriation of Meister Eckhart

The apophatic depths of divinity and psyche point to the emergence of both from that formless nothingness, that absolute silence, peace and rest, which has no frantic urge for expression but from which all expression comes. The term "apophatic" is used by theologians and religionists to describe especially the experience of the mystic who loses personal identity in a divinity which loses its personal divinity in the mystic. In this sense, a serious engagement with Jung's psychology comes in the end to nothing—to that pleromatic nothingness from which all form and consciousness derive. And once derived, only through reimmersion in such nothingness can any mind or self-understanding be renewed and broadened in its empathies. It was their familiarity with the pleroma from which both mind and its most powerful expressions emerge that drew Jung to the mystics.

As the last chapter suggests, Jung was strongly drawn to shamanic and mystical experience because both were cherished expressions of humanity's immediate and powerful experience of the archetypal dimension of the psyche. He could not be more candid on this than when he writes:

> Mystics are people who have a particularly vivid experience of the processes of the collective unconscious. Mystical experience is experience of archetypes.[272]

He makes this even clearer when he goes on to confess that he could not distinguish mystical from archetypal imagery and, by extension, the experience behind the imagery from mystical experience.[273]

Though they fascinated Jung, there are great difficulties in treating of mystics and their experience in a responsible manner. The difficulties follow from the great variety of their experience and its expression in the voluminous writings the mystics have left us. This diversity is apparent even in those Western mystics Jung cites so frequently throughout his writings.

---

272. "The Tavistock Lectures," *The Symbolic Life,* CW 18, par. 218.
273. Ibid., par. 220.

Thus Hildegarde of Bingen was a visionary, one might say a fluent hallucinator, whose writings and the art which illustrates them express her hallucinatory experience. This very format was insisted upon by the voice which ordered her to "speak and write what you see and hear."[274]

Others, such as Mechthilde of Magdeburg and the early Beguines, are less obviously given to hallucinatory experience and more to a rich imaginal life centering on such powerful imagery as a fully sexual love tryst with a youthful Christ figure. Jacob Boehme's writings are alive with imagery that forces comparison with the peculiar intensities of William Blake's art and poetry. The clarity, power and wealth of imagery in this kind of experience would serve to corroborate Jung's observation that the mystics have had intense experiences of archetypal powers which invest their imagery with a numinosity undimmed by time.

In some tension, if not open contradiction, with such profuse imagery, stands another genre of mystical experience which holds the image up to suspicion or even contempt. Such experience seems more intent on moving to the imageless ground from which all imagery comes. In that ground the experience would culminate in a total loss of identity through immersion in the unimaged, indeed unimaginable, source of all. In a religious idiom this would point to an identity of the being of the mystic and the being of God, which, again paradoxically, means the death of experience since experience as we know it demands a subject over against the object . This aspect of mystical experience reaches its apogee in Meister Eckhart, to whom Jung turned for personal spiritual sustenance and in whose experience he recognized the natural intimacy and connectedness of human consciousness with that nothingness from which all consciousness derives.

It is not difficult to prove that Jung was influenced by Meister Eckhart. In his *Collected Works* and published letters, he cites Eckhart thirty-eight times from twenty-one widely varying sources in the translation of Franz Pfeiffer's nineteenth-century collection of Eckhart's works.[275] Further, Jung cites Eckhart twice in *Memories, Dreams, Reflections*. In the first reference he pays tribute to Eckhart as the source of youthful inspiration in matters religious and philosophical. He writes, "Only in Meister Eckhart did I feel the breath of life," and then adds out of a sense of the limitations

---

274. Hildegarde of Bingen, *Scivias*, trans. Bruce Hozeski (Santa Fe: Bear and Company, 1986), p. 1.
275. *Meister Eckhart*, ed. Franz Pfeiffer, Leipzig, 1857, trans. C. de B. Evans, 2 vols. (London: John M. Watkins, 1924).

of his early scholarly pretensions, "not that I understood him."[276] In the second more telling citation Jung refers to Eckhart out of a concern that came increasingly to the fore in Jung's mature reflection. Here Jung casts Eckhart as a peripheral figure whose rejected experience and spirit, along with that of other mystics, contributed greatly to the lack of development of the Christian myth in its historical unfolding. The exclusion of Eckhart's experience and that of like spirits becomes for Jung a major factor in Christianity's current spiritual sterility.[277]

The implication of these passages is that the severing of the mind from that rootedness in the divine at the heart of mystical experience killed or maimed both religion and the culture it informed, to the detriment of both. Hence Jung's appreciation of Eckhart's experience would be the ultimate counter to the one-sided consciousness so destructively prominent in his father's religious tragedy, because Eckhart's experience culminates in unqualified unity between the human and divine.

Thus Jung was no casual reader of Eckhart. One has the impression that he almost uncannily perceived in Eckhart's corpus expressions of the deeper psyche that only someone with Jung's sensitivity to the unconscious could so readily and unerringly extract from such a mass of material. It is as Jung claims. In his appropriation of Eckhart, spirit cries out to spirit over a gap of six centuries. For Eckhart is the man to whom Jung attributes a premonitory experience of what Jung was to term the Self six hundred years before Western culture could bring it to conscious formulation in depth psychology:

> Well might the writings of this Master lie buried for six hundred years, for "his time was not yet come." Only in the nineteenth century did he find a public at all capable of appreciating the grandeur of his mind.[278]

This is the man Jung claims helped him to appreciate and practice "letting go"—in German *gelassenheit*, in traditional religious language "resignation," and in a more Heideggerian idiom "releasement." Both Jung and Eckhart understood this "letting go" or "letting be" as a certain renewing passivity which allowed the power of God or psyche, infinitely transcending the ego yet continuous with it, to work the latter's renewal in

---

276. *Memories, Dreams, Reflections*, pp. 68-69.
277. Ibid., p. 332. In this passage Jung links Meister Eckhart with Gioacchino da Fiore and Jacob Boehme as also denied a hearing in the West.
278. "Gnostic Symbols of the Self," *Aion*, CW 9ii, par. 302.

finitude from beyond the confines of the finite.[279] This sense of release from finitude's confinements springs from the experience of total immersion in that divine source which paradoxically is wholly divested of any need to act or express itself beyond itself and yet is the ultimate source of all that becomes real and distinct in finitude.

Eckhart is also the man who impressed Jung so deeply with the theme repeated throughout his work, that suffering is the swiftest way to perfection even when that suffering took the form of moral failure.[280] In his appropriation of this side of Eckhart's thought, Jung may have found remote foundations for that aspect of his psychology which would value moral failure not in and of itself but as a dramatic statement of the shadow breaking destructively into a life from which it had been excluded, in favor of a purely conscious and willful moral perfectionism. For Jung, then, borrowing from Eckhart, reflection on the pain of moral defeat becomes the occasion for self-knowledge and a more humane acceptance of self and other that only the humiliation of failure can provoke.

Before launching into a more detailed analysis of the Jung-Eckhart interface, a brief historical sketch of Eckhart's life will help the reader.

He was born in the German province of Thuringia around 1260 in one of two towns called Hockheim, one near Erfurt, and one near Gotha. In his mid teens Eckhart entered the Dominican novitiate. At the age of seventeen he was a student of arts and a Dominican studying at the University of Paris. It did not take long for the order to recognize his academic capacities. He continued his studies in Cologne in 1280, possibly under Albert the Great, Aquinas's teacher, thought by some, including Jung, to have been a familiar of alchemy.[281] In 1293-94 Eckhart was back in Paris lecturing on the Sentences of Peter Lombard, a condition then for the Master's degree.

At this point in his career a second major capacity, that of administrator, becomes apparent. Sometime prior to 1300 he was named Prior of the Dominican house in Erfurt and Vicar-Provincial of Thuringia. In 1303 he was to become Provincial of Saxony, and in 1307 was offered a second

---

279. "Commentary on 'The Secret of the Golden Flower,' " *Alchemical Studies,* CW 13, par. 20; *Mysterium Coniunctionis,* CW 14, par. 258.

280. *C.G. Jung Letters,* vol. 2, Anonymous, April 28, 1955, p. 248; Anonymous, June 28, 1956, p. 311; *Psychological Types,* CW 6, pars. 411, 415.

281. See "The Sign of the Fishes," *Aion,* CW 9ii, par. 143. Here Jung also relates Thomas Aquinas to the alchemical tradition, a rather dubious connection.

province. This engagement with the world throughout his career is worthy of note in allaying the misconception that those whose experience is as deep as Eckhart's are somehow withdrawn from life and its demands. It simply is not true of Eckhart nor of other authentic mystics.

In 1302 Eckhart received the degree of Master of Theology from Paris University. He taught there till 1303, and again from 1311-1313. During his periods of teaching Eckhart authored tracts on various theological subjects written in the best of scholastic Latin and using the very formal mode of argumentation that attached to scholasticism. Though many of the propositions that were to be later condemned were extracts from his Latin tracts, it was not really till he started yet a third career as a distinguished preacher that questions of his orthodoxy arose.

The transition began when he was transferred to the Dominican house in Strassbourg in 1314 and began combining preaching with teaching. His preaching eventually made him famous (or infamous, depending on one's theological tastes). After a further move up the Rhine to the Dominican house of studies in Cologne, his preaching to lay people and to communities of sisters drew the attention of the Franciscan Archbishop of Cologne, Henry of Virnberg, a noted heresy hunter. In 1326 Henry sponsored an initial heresy trial, after a Dominican papal investigator had cleared Eckhart. In 1326 Eckhart defended himself against various lists of statements of questionable orthodoxy extracted from both his Latin and German works. Early in 1327 Eckhart denied the canonicity, that is, the ecclesial legality of the proceedings against him in Cologne and appealed to the Apostolic See, the papacy, then resident in Avignon. In February, 1327, he defended himself publicly in the Dominican church in Cologne and some time after left for Avignon to have his case heard there.

Sometime between February 13, 1327, and April 30, 1328, he died at a place unknown while the trial was in process. The latter date is fixed in a letter sent by Pope John XX to Henry, the Archbishop of Cologne, assuring him that Eckhart's trial was continuing after the latter's death. On March 27, 1329, the bull of condemnation, "In agro dominico," lists twenty-eight propositions of which seventeen are described as heresy and eleven are suspect though capable of bearing an orthodox meaning with proper interpretation.[282] The bull mentions that Eckhart had retracted prior

---

282. The bull is to be found in English in *Meister Eckhart*, trans. Edmund Colledge and Bernard McGinn (New York: Paulist Press, 1981), pp. 77-81.

to his death all error attached to the propositions.

In the wake of his condemnation Eckhart became a peripheral figure for five to six centuries. His disciples Johan Tauler and Heinrich Suso tried to keep alive a moderate or orthodox version of his views. Luther read Tauler and may have read Eckhart in Tauler's works. Only in the nineteenth century, in German romanticism and idealism, did Eckhart enjoy a certain revival to which Jung may be referring in the above citation to the effect that Eckhart was centuries before his time. Franz Baader introduced him to Hegel who mentions him in his *Philosophy of Religion*. With Pfeiffer's nineteenth-century publication of his German works fresh dispute erupted over his orthodoxy. Many pointed to an undeniable pantheism at the core of his thought and to an overemphasis on a symbolic understanding of religious truths. Others, especially nineteenth-century neo-Thomists, encouraged by the recovery of his Latin manuscripts, tried to depict him as both orthodox and Aristotelian. Modern scholarship would deny the latter and at least question the former. Today his connections with Heidegger's mysticism[283] and the Zen tradition[284] are the foci of investigation.

Behind the frequency of Jung's references to Eckhart, one suspects lie deeper issues. These issues bear directly on the much wider implications of the psychological hermeneutic Jung brings to bear not only on Eckhart but on mystical experience as such. Jung's argument has already been made to the effect that mystics experience the numinosity of the archetypal world without mediation and so with that intensity of experience which gives rise to religion both personally and in the collective. Thus from a Jungian perspective the study of mystical experience becomes at once the study of the deeper energies and movements of the psyche, themselves the source of humanity's ineradicable religiosity and, by implication, of whatever positive contribution religion might have to make to humanity.

This characteristically Jungian hermeneutic is a two-edged sword. On the one hand Jungian interpretative resources can illuminate mystical experience by showing it to be grounded in and expressive of the deepest movements of the psyche. In so doing, Jung performs a valuable service to the contemporary world. For he makes such potentially valuable experience psychologically credible and so available to the ever-increasing army

---

283. John D. Caputo, *The Mystical Elements in Heidegger's Thought* (Athens, OH: Ohio University Press, 1984).

284. Reiner Schurmann, *Meister Eckhart*, "Appendix: Meister Eckhart and Zen Buddhism" (Bloomington: Indiana University Press, 1972), pp. 221-226.

of religiously dispossessed and institutionally disenchanted. This perspective on mystical experience could open it up as a living option to a constituency which may rightly be highly suspicious of the current pathologizing effects of formal religion and yet be in dire need of the energies the institution, when operating well, can offer the human condition. Universalizing and privatizing mystical experience by removing it from ecclesial mediation could thus extend its healing power to those who can no longer tolerate ecclesial affiliation. This process would benefit the individual greatly and would never be without wider societal effect, in spite of the protestations of those employed by various gracing cartels, because of the more benign consciousness such experience would sponsor wherever it occurs.

On the other hand, an examination of mystical experience understood as a manifestation of the ground movements of the psyche can reveal to the psychologist dimensions of the psyche which, though universal human propensities, can with difficulty be included in existing paradigms or models of psychic life.

In the interface of Jung and Eckhart both sides of this process seem to be operative. Jung uses Eckhart and other mystics to illustrate and to corroborate his understanding of the deeper movements of psychic life with profound consequences for the imagining of the divine-human relationship. But Eckhart, speaking in a religious and theological idiom, may also point to depths of the psyche which Jung, in his admiration of Eckhart, obviously could appreciate but with difficulty integrate fully into his model of the psyche. Thus we come to see what Jung's psychology reveals about the human soul and its movements through its appreciation of mystical experience. But at the same time mysticism, and especially Eckhart's, can reveal the possibility of a deeper stratum of the psyche which may evade and in some sense surpass the model of the psyche Jung has left us.

There are three places in Jung's work where his appropriation of Eckhart is particularly evident. In *Psychological Types* he uses Eckhart to illustrate his understanding of the relativity of God and to help in his formulation of the ground movement of psychic energies.[285] In *Aion* he associates Eckhart with gnostic thought.[286] In *Psychology and Religion* he relates Eckhart to Zen in the context of the individual's immediate and imageless access to the ground of truth and life, the matrix of consciousness,

---

285. "The Relativity of the God-Concept in Meister Eckhart," CW 6, pp. 241ff.
286. "Gnostic Symbols of the Self," CW 9ii, par. 301.

within the psyche.[287]

Psychological Types is Jung's first work after his break with Freud. In it Jung looks for models of religious experience that would help him come to terms with his own frightening and immediate experience of the powers of the unconscious, and which would be helpful in the formulation of his own still developing understanding of the psyche.[288] A major feature of this new understanding is what he calls the relativity of God. The meaning of relativity in this context does not, as such, refer to the value of relativism endemic to Jung's understanding of archetypal expressions and so of the religions (addressed above in chapter three). Rather here Jung's understanding entails a radically new paradigm which would insist that God and human consciousness are so intimately—I would suggest ontologically—linked that they are best understood as "functions" of each other.

This intimacy supposes a mutual dependence and interaction which might accurately be described by both Eckhart and Jung as a process of mutual redemption. Thus the idea of a God who is wholly other than humanity, and in principle separable from human consciousness, is denied by Jung in this early work and throughout the remainder of his corpus. More, Jung's reconception of divinity's relation to humanity would deny to divinity a unilateral and unforced activity in either creation or redemptive forays into human history. Rather this newer paradigm necessarily implies the creation of human consciousness as the needed cooperant on whom divinity is dependent for divinity's redemption in the human. Jung makes these positions clear when he writes:

> The "relativity of God," as I understand it, denotes a point of view that does not conceive of God as "absolute," i.e., wholly "cut off" from man and existing outside and beyond all human conditions, but as in a certain sense dependent on him; it also implies a reciprocal and essential relation between man and God, whereby man can be understood as a function of God, and God as a psychological function of man.[289]

Later in this passage Jung writes, again explicitly but now more aggressively, that the God who is understood as a metaphysical absolute and

---

287. "Foreword to Suzuki's 'Introduction to Zen Buddhism,' " CW 11, pars. 887-888, 893.
288. See *Memories, Dreams, Reflections*, chapter 6, "Confrontation with the Unconscious," pp. 170ff.
289. *Psychological Types*, CW 6, par. 412.

not as a "function of the unconscious" points to an unconscious religious or theological mind whose most characteristic trait is "a complete unawareness of the fact that God's action springs from one's own inner being."[290]

Jung goes on to clarify precisely what he means in his conception of divinity and humanity as functions of each other. First he pays Eckhart high tribute as having been among the first to realize that the human experience of God originates wholly from within the psyche, though obviously from a source transcendent to the ego. Jung also makes here an early statement of a foundational element in his psychology as it touches religion, namely, that to attribute humanity's experience of God to an extrapsychic agency is a profound form of unconsciousness. This would mean that conceptions of divinity as "wholly other" than the human are unconscious of the origin of the sense of God in the psyche and of the projection under which they labor when they base their theological and spiritual life on such projections.

In these lines Jung indicts all theologies and spiritualities based on transcendental monotheisms of being unconscious themselves and so of promoting unconsciousness because they remain unaware of the origin of their diverse "one and only" Gods in the unconscious. Needless to say such religious perspectives would hardly be up to what Jung describes as the most pressing psycho-spiritual task of modernity, namely, the internalization of these now competing *monotheoi* in the name of human survival and well-being.

Consistent with the above foundational themes, Jung goes on to elaborate the implications of this insight in terms of the psychological consequences of the withdrawal of the projection of the Gods and their psychic internalization. The operative passage that Jung uses from Eckhart in this discussion reads, "The soul is not blissful because she is in God, she is blissful because God is in her."[291] Jung uses the passage to show in terms of his understanding of psychic energy how the soul loses her bliss when she is in God and how she recovers her bliss when God is in her.

Jung describes two distinct modes in which the soul can be in God and so forego its bliss. In the first instance the soul projects the energies that give rise to the sense of God onto some external object or person. An example of the former would be a theological doctrine like that of Catholic

290. Ibid., par. 413.
291. Ibid., par. 418.

ancient

transubstantiation where bread and wine are considered to be divine. Obviously the basis for such a hoary belief is the inability of the mind to understand presence in anything other than a physical, literal mode.[292] As we have seen in chapter five, the projection of the sacred can also have a person as its object. This process describes the primitive psychology of *tondi* or *mana* in which the divine energy that belongs to the individual is projected onto someone or something.[293] The previous chapter has shown how such projections work in such disparate phenomena as the creation of the shaman or the modern papacy, and what consequences of freedom and moral responsibility would attend their withdrawal.

The recovery of such primordial projection is for the individual always the recovery of the energy that had been given away in the creation of the divine reality beyond oneself, to which the victim usually gave an unqualified and unseemly obeisance. This is well described by Jung when he writes, "The power that rules us is outside, in the external world, and through it alone are we permitted to live."[294] The withdrawal of the projection places God back in the soul, with the bliss attendant to the self-possession and assurance characteristic of a consciousness living out of its internalized divinity now in the service of the soul and no longer as its external oppressor.

But Jung's second sense of the soul's moving from a state of a blissless being in God to the bliss of God being in it is far more complex. This is because it describes a wholly internal process in which the soul moving into the well-spring of all life within the psyche stands in danger of being overwhelmed by what Jung calls the creative *dynamis* of this inner source itself. In describing this danger Jung is striving to depict a psychic situation in which the soul could be drowned in the creative potential of the deeper unconscious, were it not able to establish its own autonomy and mediate the creativity of the depths of the psyche to the ego. Jung describes both the hazards of this psychic situation and its ideal resolution in Eckhart's terms:

> When, says Eckhart, the soul is in God it is not "blissful," for when this organ of perception is overwhelmed by the divine *dynamis* it is by no means a happy state. But when God is in the soul, i.e., when the soul be-

292. See Jung's discussion of the historical origins of the doctrine of transubstantiation and the Radbertus-Scotus Erigina debate, ibid., pars. 35-39.
293. Ibid., par. 417.
294. "Archaic Man," *Civilization in Transition,* CW 10, par. 138.

comes a vessel for the unconscious and makes itself an image or symbol of it, this is a truly happy state.[295]

What Jung is here describing, using Eckhart's religious imagery of the birth of God in the soul,[296] becomes the ground movement of psychic energies in his own psychological paradigm. The dynamic is that of a rhythmic and repeated immersion of the ego and its energies into and out of the source of all energies in the deeper psyche. In these passages Jung describes this movement of psychic energies as analogous to the diastolic and systolic movement of blood into and out of the heart.[297] Both sides of the movement are essential to health. The failure of either is fatal.

As appropriated by Jung, this psychic circularity means that the soul must enter into, or allow to enter into it, the deeper and divine energies of the unconscious which it in turn mediates to consciousness. Ideally in this circular movement the soul mediates to consciousness the energies she herself derives from the deeper unconscious in a hopefully ongoing and ever surer rhythm. Could the soul not enter or mediate these energies to the ego, the ego would wither in a sterile desert of barren consciousness. This condition remains for Jung the core pathology of patriarchy. Hence Jung's psychology extends patriarchal pathology beyond a constrictive and naive gender basis. Jung identifies the patriarchal blight with the pathology of that consciousness afflicting members of either gender who have lost their vital resonance with the energies of the unconscious.

On the other hand, were the soul to drown in these energies the ego would drown with it, in what Jung calls "the immersion in the 'flood and source.' "[298] Jung does realize that such an immersion in the root source of all energy relates rather closely to that state of consciousness (or its absence) which Eckhart sought to depict in what he called his experience of breakthrough. However Jung's understanding of this moment of immersion within the total dynamic of psychic renewal, as well as Eckhart's very active life, clearly demand that if such regression to an unqualified identity with God is not completed by a return to a consciousness enhanced by the experience of self-loss, then unity with God would be akin to a catatonia,

---

295. *Psychological Types*, par. 425.
296. Ibid. Jung here cites a passage in Eckhart to the effect that the purpose of the virtuous life and the Incarnation is God's birth in the soul and the soul's birth in God.
297. Ibid., par. 428.
298. Ibid., par. 430.

the permanent death of the ego.

Thus the perils of establishing a healthy commerce with the deeper levels of the unconscious belong to all of psychic life and spiritual maturation. Jung is here using Eckhart's religious expression as a dramatic instance of what is at stake in the negotiations between consciousness and the unconscious, between God and the human, as functions of each other in every life. Not to experience one's native point of unity with deity is desiccating and debilitating; to identify with it is death.

From this point Jung moves quickly to the dialectic at the heart of his and Eckhart's thought. The soul which is in some sense the creature of God is also needed by God to mediate God's energies to consciousness. In this role she is the mother of God as the vehicle through which God becomes conscious in human consciousness. This reciprocity between soul and God is the basis of the psychological universality which Jung gives to the central theme in Eckhart's thought, God's birth in the soul. This psychological movement is also the basis of the virgin birth taken literally and historically in much of Christianity's response to its myth. Contradicting Christian historical literalism, Jung and Eckhart would contend that Mary's virgin birth is a symbol for processes of psychological and spiritual maturation which are universal and true of both genders.

The understanding of the birth of God in the soul as a psychological event rhythmically repeated would also provide the basis for the assertion by Eckhart and other mystics that God seeks to be born again and again in the soul. This divine lust is an expression of the divine interest and that of the unconscious in becoming as fully conscious as possible through the mediating function of the soul, in such a way as to complete divinity in the completion of human consciousness. Jung sums this up in his own terms: "Here Eckhart states bluntly that God is dependent on the soul, and at the same time, that the soul is the birthplace of God."[299]

Let us now turn to the second appearance of Eckhart in Jung's work. From what has been said it is not surprising that Jung associates Eckhart's experience with gnosticism. He does so because of the gnostic experience of a power in whom all opposites are one, a power which precedes all differentiation and yet in which all differentiation is latent, the famous pleroma of Jung's *Seven Sermons to the Dead.*[300] This dimension of the psy-

---

299. Ibid., par. 426.
300. *Memories, Dreams, Reflections*, pp. 378f.

che Jung relates to Eckhart's experience of the Godhead in what Eckhart calls the "breakthrough," an experience in which all differentiation in God and between God and creature is dissolved.[301]

Jung writes accurately, though with that same sense of paradox characteristic of Eckhart himself, that such an experience would cause unconsciousness in anyone who would undergo it, since all consciousness is related to differentiation, especially between subject and object, and there is none in this dimension of the psyche. In a line Eckhart would enjoy Jung writes, "As the Godhead is essentially unconscious, so too is the man who lives in God."[302] This is but a reference to what has been discussed above as the absence of bliss in that ego which is wholly dissolved in divinity. However, the moment of loss of all differentiation would appear to be for Eckhart, Jung and the gnostics the most complete union with God from which one hopefully returns remade to the world.

Indeed, Eckhart's understanding of true poverty and humility rests on a total immersion and self-loss in this dimension of being. In this sense the ultimate act of humility is attained in one's unqualified recovery of and union with one's native divinity. But one must then return from it, and as one does the reality of God is born again in the soul and empowers the individual for life in the finite world. With Jung the repetitive, incestuous and circular movement of the soul into this pleroma and back to consciousness is the base meaning of incarnation and of individuation. It is of interest to note that by linking Eckhart with gnostic experience Jung would imply that gnostic and mystic—and by extension alchemist and shaman— draw their experience from the same deep wells of the psyche.

In his third major reference to Eckhart the same themes are operative when Jung links Eckhart with the satori experience of the Zen tradition.[303] Here Jung deals with Eckhart and Zen as spiritualities of immediacy. He goes on to contrast such spiritualities to those offering access to the unconscious either through a set of archetypal images other than one's own, as is the case in the Ignatian exercises, or through ecclesial mediation based on the liturgical manipulation of archetypal energies in the eliciting of expected communal response, as in traditional church services.[304]

---

301. "Gnostic Symbols of the Self," *Aion,* CW 9ii, par. 301.
302. Ibid.
303. "Foreword to Suzuki's 'Introduction to Zen Buddhism,' " *Psychology and Religion,* CW 11, par. 887.
304. Ibid., par. 893.

Jung is here directing attention to the possibility of an unmediated access to those layers of one's psyche which precede images and from which all images flow into consciousness. Again the implication is that the deeper one moves into one's interiority the more one draws near the imageless ground of all imagery. Later in this section, Jung identifies this ground with what he calls the matrix mind, and describes it as the source not only of all imagery but of all the disciplines and forms of expression of which the conscious mind is capable.[305]

Before leaving Jung's treatment of Eckhart, a moment should be devoted to his interest in some material that may be apocryphal. One such story has to do with the appearance of a little naked boy to Eckhart. Jung interprets this as a symbol of the divine child at work in Eckhart's psyche, and in one instance sees the child as symbolizing that rootedness in the past, indeed in eternity, that enables one to move into the future without debilitating self-loss, especially in times of stressful change.[306]

Given Eckhart's difficult historical role of ushering in a fragile consciousness destined to prevail but deemed heretical by his contemporaries, one can appreciate the grounding and stabilizing role of the image of the divine child, the Self, in his conflict-filled life. Jung argues that the energy carried by the symbol enabled Eckhart to bear the weight of the future out of what he felt to be fidelity both to the depth of his own experience and to his Christian past. In this context the image of the child becomes an image of support to all those caught in the suffering realization that one's tradition must undergo transformations in the interests of its own survival and its continuing capacity to mediate life, and that these transformations, at least initially, are likely to be rejected by the tradition itself.

Jung was also fascinated by the tale of Eckhart's daughter who reportedly described herself as not imbued with any feminine or masculine role but, because identified with none, possessed of all.[307] Jung marvels at such a woman as an image of Eckhart's anima. But he could as well have seen in her a powerful and many-faced wisdom figure not unlike the gnostic Sophia. Spirits attracted to such a figure would be interested in sides of the feminine and masculine not easily confined to moral approval.

A final possibly apocryphal figure in the Eckhart corpus to whom Jung

---

305. Ibid., par. 899.
306. "The Psychology of the Child Archetype," *The Archetypes and the Collective Unconscious,* CW 9i, pars. 267-268.
307. *Mysterium Coniunctionis*, CW 14, par.102.

never refers but whom he surely would have appreciated is the figure of Sister Katerina.[308] She appears initially as a penitent and seeker whose spiritual development gradually outstrips that of her clerical director. In the end she achieves a state of spiritual maturity which she forbids to him as beyond his current maturity. Such an advanced stage of spiritual development enables her to say with a powerful simplicity to the man she has surpassed, "Sir, rejoice with me. I have become God."[309]

Let us turn now to a summation of the distinctive features of Eckhart's thought and the reason for its rejection by orthodoxy then and now. In dealing with the theological imagination, medieval or modern, two options are possible. One can begin with God and trace the emanation of humanity from its divine source, or one can begin with humanity and trace the way back to its origin. Let us begin our treatment of Eckhart with the first option, how he envisages the line from God to humanity.

Eckhart distinguished himself from theologians before and since by unmistakably positing a quaternity in the divine life itself. He does this by clearly distinguishing between the Godhead and its derivative, God as Trinitarian. The Godhead which precedes and gives rise to the Trinitarian God is totally without differentiation, a creative nothingness from which all differentiation proceeds, including that of the Trinity itself. Eckhart writes, "God and Godhead are as distinct as heaven and earth."[310]

Whatever experience in Eckhart's life led to his distinction between Godhead and Trinity, he has, from a Jungian perspective, recovered or discovered in the fourteenth century the deepest meaning of the Great Goddess or Great Mother. This connection between Eckhart's conception of the Godhead and Jung's of the Great Mother or Goddess is not an irresponsible conclusion. For both Jung and Eckhart this dimension of the psyche points to that generative source which is without differentiation in itself and from which all differentiation, both within and beyond divine life, derives. In Eckhart's and Jung's paradigm she must thus be under-

308. "Appendix, The Sister Catherine Treatise," trans. Elvira Borgstadt, *Meister Eckhart* (New York: Paulist Press, 1986), pp. 349-387.
309. Ibid., p. 358.
310. See Reiner Schurmann, *Meister Eckhart* (Bloomington: Indiana University Press, 1978) p. 114. The citation is from the sermon *Nolite timere eos* in Franz Pfeifer, *Deutsche Mystiker des viersehnten Jarhunderts* (Leipzig, 1857, and Aalen, 1962), vol. 2, p. 18. In the Evans translation of Franz Pfeifer, *Meister Eckhart*, it is sermon 56 and the citation appears in vol 1, p. 142. On the distinction between Godhead and Trinity see Schurmann, pp. 45-46, 114.

stood to give birth to or mother the Trinity itself. It is in cyclical reimmersion in her renewing nothingness that Eckhart locates humanity's most profound union with God.

Eckhart describes this great creative ocean out of which the Trinity emanates as in no way moved by its own dynamic to express itself beyond itself. It rests wholly content within its own immensity, the ultimate resource for "letting be" or "living without why." Writes Eckhart of this ground, "The essence of Godhead begets not."[311] His treatment of this dimension of deity, the Godhead, appears to be the basis of some tension in his thought, because obviously she did give birth first to the Trinity and through the Trinity to what is called creation. Otherwise Eckhart could not have pointed to her reality in the fourteenth century nor I to Eckhart's pointing to her reality in the twentieth. Had she not broken her containment nothing would be or all would still be nothing.

But the way that Eckhart imagines the Trinity to function when it does differentiate from its maternal precedent is of great interest and is given much attention in his condemnation. For he thinks that, once that process described as the Father's generating the Son and uniting with the Son in the Spirit begins, it necessarily flows into creation and that creation and human consciousness become a necessary continuation of the differentiation which is the life of the Trinity. The life of the Trinity, he terms a *bullitio,* an image of a boiling or seething process which culminates in a necessary *ebullitio,* a boiling over into the reality of creation.[312] In this paradigm Eckhart denies any imaginal situation in which a self-sufficient God existed in magnificent isolation from eternity. As his condemnation makes clear, he argues that God created as soon as he existed out of a divine need for humanity.[313]

Eckhart's understanding of creation's continuity with the Trinitarian process proved too intimate for orthodox ears. In one of his more striking formulations he says that in the one Word two things are spoken or that he hears two things.[314] By this he means God's expression in Trinitarian life cannot be separated from God's expression in creation since they are two

311. Evans, *Meister Eckhart*, vol. 1, sermon 58, "Divine Understanding," p. 148. This sermon may not be authentic but the citation is true to Eckhart's mind.
312. See Bernard McGinn, *Meister Eckhart* (New York: Paulist Press, 1981), "Theological Summary," pp. 31, 37-45.
313. "In agro dominico," March 27, 1329, ibid., pp. 77-78.
314. See for instance, "Commentary on John," ibid., p. 148.

aspects of one process. He thus founds his pantheism on both humanity's experience of its continuity with Trinitarian life and with the Word of God in that life. The nineteenth century defined this latter position, rightly, as panlogism, to mean that the depth structure and dynamic of all that is, and especially of the human mind, is divine.

It is in this aspect of his vision of creation flowing from its expression in divinity that Eckhart introduces a second quaternity. It is identical in function with Jung's insistence that Trinitarian models must currently cede to quaternitarian models in the interest of humanity's becoming whole by giving birth to the wholeness of God. This means with both Eckhart and Jung that religious paradigms of a discontinuous divine transcendence must cede to one in which the divine but unconscious fullness is situated in the unconscious as generative of consciousness. This divine but unconscious unity, the pleroma, embracing all the undifferentiated opposites, gives birth to consciousness as that power in which the opposites are consciously differentiated and brought into union in history.

This paradigm moves from Eckhart into modernity through Jacob Boehme and Hegel. At the heart of Boehme's mystical experience is what he saw as humanity's now dawning experience that only in human consciousness does divinity become conscious of the divine totality. This perspective means that the creator can no longer evade responsibility for anything created, nor can the human deny the divinity of what is. In Jung's hands this means that the bodily, the feminine and the demonic must be restored to their original divinity in the interests of both divine and human completion. From the human perspective it means that consciousness can no longer evade its basic task in history, that of serving as the vehicle of God's becoming fully conscious.

Eckhart goes on to challenge the Christian imagination, both medieval and modern, when he refuses to isolate the Christ figure as an individual or the meaning of Christianity as hanging on historical events. He does this by asking what good it does him if Christ is born in Mary and not in himself. And when the Word is born in his soul, Eckhart affirms—and was condemned for affirming—that the individual then is another Christ, *is* that reality in which the individual then participates.[315] This position is identical with Jung's, which would locate the true imitation of Christ, and

---

315. Evans, *Meister Eckhart*, vol. 2, p. 186. The sermon is a commentary on John 12:24.

indeed the Christ event, not in an external adherence to a past event—often imbued with a literal miraculous aura so grotesque in its uniqueness as to make the incident freakish to modern sensitivities—but rather in a psychic or interior reexperiencing of the archetypal truth of the event. Thus Eckhart's insistence that the birth of God in the soul identifies that soul with the Word of God, and so with the experienced reality of Christ, anticipates Jung's psychological formulation of the same experience six hundred years later as that of the birth of the Self in consciousness through the unity the Self works between consciousness and its divine depths.

Eckhart's treatment of the birth of God in the soul serves as the turnaround point to trace out his conception of the soul's return to God. Modern scholars now see this return centered on two distinct movements in one process, the birth of the Word in the soul and the breakthrough.[316] My own tracking of this process leads me to agree with modern commentators that what Eckhart means by the birth of God in the soul is a discrete, or, at least, distinguishable preliminary stage. For rather than immediately lead the individual in whom it happens back to the life of conscious engagement, the event serves as the occasion for yet a deeper ingression into the divine reality which Eckhart calls the breakthrough. This process involves the loss of all identity and differentiation on the part of both Trinity and humanity, in a total mutual obliteration of one in the other. If God is nothing and the individual is nothing, can they be anything but one? Thus for Eckhart the furthest reach of unity with the Godhead takes place in a complete dissolution in the Cosmic Mother.

In his imagery—which has to be self-contradictory to capture fully his sense of total ego-loss in the nothingness which mothers all—one recovers one's eternal and ineradicable truth, one's unqualified unity with deity, in a place where all differentiation is negated. Somewhat poetically, and yet precisely, Eckhart says that even God, understood as Trinitarian and so differentiated or removed from the Godhead like the creature, cannot enter this dimension of reality. In this state Eckhart identifies himself with the unmoved mover, or, in medieval terms, with God.[317] It is from this total removal from conscious life through immersion in its source that Eckhart

---

316. See John D. Caputo, *The Mystical Element in Heidegger's Thought* (Athens, Ohio: Ohio University Press, 1984), pp. 128-134; and Schurmann, *Meister Eckhart,* p.164.
317. See Evans, *Meister Eckhart,* vol. 1, p. 220, from the sermon "The Poor in Spirit."

apparently derives the energy to reengage the world. Thus in a reversal of the usual meaning of the Martha-Mary Biblical story, Eckhart reads Martha as someone whose renewal in the nothingness from which all proceeds has freed her to live a life of active service, while Mary, who has yet to experience and be transformed by these depths, must sit at the knee of the Christ figure and await the enabling experience which Martha has undergone.[318]

Let us conclude with a final comparison beginning with points of agreement between Jung and Eckhart. The basic shift of perspective in the religious paradigm of both is that God and humanity are so intimately connected that they are functions of each other. This common feature explains the profoundly pantheistic element that enlivens the thought and spirit of each and gives to them the assurance that the sense of God, in whatever form it might take, is a universal and ineradicable human capacity.

But theirs is no simple pantheism, for in the commerce between the divine and human poles of a single cosmic organism a process of mutual redemption is in progress. Both would agree that God was compelled to create humanity in order to become fully conscious in it. To this basic agreement Jung would add that a major feature in the divine compulsion is God's necessity to constellate and resolve in human consciousness the contradiction divinity itself could neither perceive nor resolve in its own life.[319]

More than this, both Eckhart and Jung describe the dynamics involved in the mutual redemption of humanity and divinity in a discernibly similar manner. For both a consciousness aware of its alienated otherness from its source reenters that source as the ground of its own interiority, and somehow moving behind the opposites which are latent in that source recovers an enhanced vitality for life. With Jung the hallmark of this reborn consciousness is its capacity to affirm and reconcile opposites in the conditions of personal and, by extension, collective life. It is difficult to escape the conclusion that this capacity to love and unite opposites is a result of an experience which had attained to the unity which precedes the oppositional and so is peculiarly invested with a love for the opposites based on an experience of their common origin. This accounts for the powers of reconciliation that frequently attach to mystical consciousness.

However, the unmediated nature of this access to the further reaches of

318. Ibid., vol. 2, pp. 90f. The sermon's is "Martha and Mary" and is authentic.
319. This is a ground theme in Jung's work but is made explicit in "Answer to Job," *Psychology and Religion,* CW 11.

humanity where it intersects without hindrance with deity can be trouble-some to orthodoxy, as it obviously was with Eckhart and to some lesser extent with Jung. The reason is that orthodoxy, as the provider of the religious ideology on which the status quo is grounded, is often imbued with a lesser vision and with a vested interest in its maintenance. Speaking of the satori experience which he relates to Eckhart's Jung writes:

> There is nothing in our civilization to foster these strivings, not even the Church, the custodian of religious values. Indeed, it is the function of the Church to oppose all original experience, because this can only be un-orthodox.[320]

Jung has contributed immensely to the modern appreciation of Eckhart by showing Eckhart's experience to be grounded in the deepest movement of the psyche toward its natural maturation, which is always for Jung intensely religious. As seen in chapter three, the innately religious nature of individuation is evident in Jung's appreciation of the master symbols of the Self. The mandala, the *anthropos*, the alchemical *unus mundus* and synchronicity all evidence a consciousness moving toward an integration of the many personal energies within the individual, running hand in hand with the integration of the individual with the totality. What apparently works this personal integration and universal relatedness is the individual's experienced unity with the ground of the totality as one's personal ground, an experience brought into high prominence in mystical experience.

Thus Jung provides us with a critical and more conscious capacity to respond to Eckhart's experience, indeed even to assimilate it personally. But in doing this Jung, like Eckhart, has moved from a Trinitarian to a quaternitarian paradigm and introduced a conception of humanity's relation to God which is abrasive to Western orthodoxy. For it clearly implies that God depends on human consciousness for a redemption lacking to the divine life in itself. This implication is hostile to traditional ideas of divine transcendence and self-sufficiency. It would demand radical recasting of such central themes as the gratuity of creation and the nature of the fall, since both men imply that the universal truth of original sin is the sin of becoming conscious. Finally, the gratuity of God in the gracing of humanity is radically compromised, in the new paradigm, through its assumption of a divine self-interest which denies that divinity could be unaffected by the outcome of the human adventure, or that divinity could become incar-

---

320. "Foreword to Suzuki's 'Introduction to Zen Buddhism,' " ibid., par. 903.

nate or conscious in humanity without humanity's cooperation.

For these reasons contemporary Jungian scholars such as Murray Stein, while clearly perceiving the implications of the shift to a quaternitarian paradigm, perceive equally clearly that it cannot be mediated or encouraged by ecclesial communities grounded on the Christian myth with its Trinitarian and self-sufficient deity.[321] Stein is very much aware that the consciousness emerging through Jung's myth supersedes Christianity as Christianity claims to have superseded its Jewish precedent and origin. Thus Eckhart's thought would appear to be as unacceptable to today's inquisitors as it was to those in the fourteenth century.

This is dramatically evident in the Vatican's silencing in 1989 of the American Dominican, Matthew Fox, for his sustained efforts to make the theology of Eckhart, his fellow Dominican, live again in the twentieth century as a significant counter to the sterility of Christian spirituality. Between Eckhart's condemnation in 1328 and Fox's in 1989, nothing has changed from the viewpoint of institutional theology, a fact all the more discouraging in the wake of the hope bred by Vatican II in the sixties.

Having looked at how Jung uses Eckhart to formulate a new understanding of the divine-human relation in terms of a modern appreciation of the life of the psyche, let us turn to what Eckhart's response, even contribution, to Jung's psychology might be.

Eckhart's work seems to point to an experience of so complete a divestiture of individuality in those realms of human interiority where humanity and divinity merge, that one is forced to wonder if he did not go deeper into the psyche than its archetypal base, where Jung, at least in his writings, felt he had struck bottom. For Jung, even in his conception of the collective unconscious, attributes to the archetypes a certain potentiality, some differentiation however latent or "contaminated," to use a Jungian phrase, which does seek further differentiation and expression in human consciousness. But one cannot avoid the feeling that Eckhart experienced some void beyond even the archetypal world in that experience he calls the breakthrough. Obviously Jung could appreciate and was manifestly aware of this dimension of reality in his linking Eckhart with Zen, and again in the work that led to his break with Freud,[322] where the image of the unconscious as oceanic comes to the fore as it does in some of his alchemical

---

321. *Jung's Treatment of Christianity*, chapter 5, especially pp. 185-186.
322. *Symbols of Transformation*, CW 5.

imagery. But the experience of so radical a self-loss is only questionably a component of Jung's model of the psyche and its working.

Speculating on this point, one might wonder if it has something to do with the terror that attached to Jung's first experience of the deep unconscious and its powers in the painful period following his break with Freud.[323] It may have left him with a residual fear of, and certainly an abiding respect for, the potentially devouring powers of that infinite abyss beneath every center of consciousness where Eckhart apparently felt so much at home. Although time has closed over the possibility of recovering the personal experience that lies behind the heritage Eckhart left us, Jung himself would claim that such speculation is far from idle and that we neglect it at our peril. He writes:

> These considerations have made me extremely cautious in my approach to the further metaphysical significance that may possibly underlie archetypal statements. There is nothing to stop their ultimate ramifications from penetrating to the very ground of the universe. We alone are the dumb ones if we fail to notice it.[324]

The reason Jung felt that it would be "dumb" to refuse to pursue the implications of archetypal experience is one shared by Eckhart. For both, the depth of the penetration of human interiority is directly proportionate to the benefits brought back: a renewal of the zest for a life balanced in itself and moving to an extended and unqualified embrace of humanity in all its expressions. Such an extended embrace is made possible through contact with the one source of the glorious human multiplicity dwelling in the depth of every single human being and longing to become conscious.

Out of the intensity of this experience in his own life, Jung would gladly join in Eckhart's most paradoxical prayer, "I pray to God to rid me of God."[325] For both were confident that when lesser and divisive faiths and forms of consciousness are lost, the loser is freer, the rest of us safer and the community richer in every way.

---

323. See above, note 279.
324. "A Psychological Approach to the Dogma of the Trinity," *Psychology and Religion,* CW 11, par. 295.
325. From "Blessed are the Poor," Schurmann, *Meister Eckhart,* pp. 216, 219.

Afterword

Until not long ago the religions could still present themselves as somehow saving humanity. Today a fearful and much more sober humanity asks how it can be saved from its religions. In the face of religion's historical performance the question must arise, "If atheism were possible would it not be morally demanded?"

Jung's psychology has helped both in constellating a consciousness critical of religion's track record and in suggesting strategies of response. His psychology has contributed to the ability to ask of religion what the law asks about pornography: "Does it have a redeeming social value?"

Jung's psychology has contributed to this sharpened critique of religion by identifying its generative source in the archetypal power of the unconscious and showing so clearly how these powers can grip consciousness and deprive it of freedom and dignity. Thus Jung has alerted us to the potentially terminal, or terminating, shadow side of faith in religious or political guise. The realization is now more widespread that those committed in faith should often be committed.

And yet the perceptive reader will by now understand the deceptive implication in the title of this work. For, while there may be strategies for the loss of faith, they can never achieve, sadly, more than partial success. On the impossibility of the loss of faith by existential humanity Jung would agree fully with Tillich's comment: "Our ultimate concern can destroy us as it can heal us. But we can never be without it."[326] And here the other side of Jung's understanding of the psyche comes into play. By showing the religion-making propensities of the psyche to be native to our humanity, the possibility of the loss of faith is not a real one. The final question then becomes, "How can humanity deal with its inescapable faith-engendering facility without being destroyed by it?"

All that Jung offers, and it may be as much as can be offered, is the suggestion that the individual stay in conscious dialogue with that inner power which is the source of the world's religions. Perhaps the only hope in the end is the inner dialogue carried on on behalf of the emergence of the safer myth. Jung valued the individual's contribution to its emergence as

---

326. Paul Tillich, *Dynamics of Faith*, p. 16.

the greatest contribution one could make to humanity. More, Jung implies that fidelity to this inner voice is fidelity to a power whose ultimate intent is personal vitality, the integration of the individual's multiplicity through the balance of inner opposites, and a progressively extended empathy for the world beyond.

It is easy to pay lip service to these values which Jung felt were basic to psychological and religious maturation, far too easy when it is realized that their incarnation so often entails the loss of the faith that stands in their way. This form of suffering is frequently disguised in an attraction to the values of Jungian psychology that, ironically, is evident in the fascination with his work by Christians. Such a flirtation with Jungian psychology can no longer conceal its own motivation, which is the unacknowledged fact that traditional Christian spirituality is currently dysfunctional. The oft unspoken hope is that Jungian psychology can become a factor in its revalidation. But even the Scriptures of a dying myth warn that the dead should bury the dead (Matt. 8.22) and that new wine cannot be poured into old wineskins (Matt. 9:17).

In this sense Jungian psychology defies manipulation in the interests of the renewal of any religious ideology. On the contrary, it holds out to the Christian or devotee of any stripe not the possibility of the revitalization of the dead but rather a surpassing compensation which would function with the force of a new revelation or dispensation. In the final analysis, there are few if any of the ground values of Jungian psychology to be found in the Biblical "good news." It is little wonder, then, that Jungian psychology is good news to those who have suffered so long from bad news in their own traditions.

If the values of Jung's good news are to be significantly realized, then the religious horsemen of death must first be faced. Jung fingers them. They are faith, hope and charity clothed in religious or political certitude riding on behalf of the death they so gloriously seek in the name of their disparate revelations. If these enemies of humanity can be unhorsed internally, that personal wholeness and wider compassion which draws so many to Jung's psychology may surface. But their unhorsing is no easy task, especially when it is remembered that they ride unchecked unless undone in the inner world from which they unleash their death on the outer.

Jung could hardly have delineated the dilemma more precisely or in greater detail. The ball is now in our court.

Index

absolute faith, 68
Absolute Other, 35
Acton, Lord, 103
Aion, 120
alchemy, 20, 50, 51, 56-57, 92, 106-
    108
American Revolution, 66
analogia entis, 86
analysis: 90-91
    as shamanism, 97
anima, 12, 127
anima mundi, 47
Anselm, 45
"Answer to Job," 8, 23, 25-26, 40, 84
anthropos, 48-49
anti-Semitism, 65
apocalypticism, 26-27, 67, 70-72
apocatastasis, 93
Aquinas, 79, 86
archaic man, 99-101, 104
archetypal energies: 53, 66, 76, 97-98
    as creator of religion, 61, 63
    basis in collective unconscious, 59
archetypes: 12, 22, 24, 33, 35-36, 134
    symbolic expression of, 58-59
asceticism, 91
atheism, 82
Augustine, 45
ayami, 106

baptism, 59
Barth, Karl, 80-81
Bible, 15, 22, 29, 54, 137
Boehme, Jacob, 68-69, 83, 115, 130
Bonaventure, 47, 77, 79, 86
breakthrough (Eckhart), 124, 126, 131,
    134

Buber, Martin, 30-37, 41
Carpocrates, 32
Catholicism *(see also* papacy, Vatican
    I, Vatican II), 10, 103-104, 110-
    111
celibacy of priesthood, 10
Christ: birth in the soul, 130-131
    as God's final revelation, 8, 111
    as historical figure, 54, 79, 91, 130-
    131
    Incarnation of, 25, 77-78, 86-87
    perfection of, 11, 38, 39
    suffering of, 25-26
    as symbol, 21, 62, 71, 102
Christianity: gnostic tradition in, 29,
    56
    Jung's critique of, 80 and *passim*
    Jung's psychology as countermyth
        to, 7-9, 12, 20, 24-26, 62, 75
    one-sidedness of, 40, 88-89, 94
    perspective on split between good
        and evil, 27, 38, 39
    a spiritual religion, 91
    view of God's motive for creation,
        85-86
clock symbol, 51-52
collective unconscious: 11, 33, 90, 97
    as source of religions, 60, 112
coniunctio, 20-21
consciousness: 11-12, 19, 65, 130, 132
    death of, 25
    dialogue with the unconscious, 68,
        73-74, 89-91
    evolution of, 87
    resolution of Divine contradictions
        in, 19-20, 23-28, 39-41, 55-56,
        83-86, 132

138

Studies in Jungian Psychology by Jungian Analysts

Sewn Paperbacks

Getting To Know You: The Inside Out of Relationship
Daryl Sharp ISBN 0-919123-56-2. 128 pp. $15

Eros and Pathos: Shades of Love and Suffering
Aldo Carotenuto ISBN 0-919123-39-2. 144 pp. $15

Descent to the Goddess: A Way of Initiation for Women
Sylvia Brinton Perera ISBN 0-919123-05-8. 112 pp. $14

Addiction to Perfection: The Still Unravished Bride
Marion Woodman ISBN 0-919123-11-2. Illustrated. 208 pp. $17pb/$20hc

The Creation of Consciousness: Jung's Myth for Modern Man
Edward F. Edinger ISBN 0-919123-13-9. Illustrated. 128 pp. $14

The Illness That We Are: A Jungian Critique of Christianity
John P. Dourley ISBN 0-919123-16-3. 128 pp. $14

The Pregnant Virgin: A Process of Psychological Transformation
Marion Woodman ISBN 0-919123-20-1. Illustrated. 208 pp. $17pb/$20hc

The Jungian Experience: Analysis and Individuation
James A. Hall, M.D. ISBN 0-919123-25-2. 176 pp. $16

Phallos: Sacred Image of the Masculine
Eugene Monick ISBN 0-919123-26-0. 30 illustrations. 144 pp. $15

The Christian Archetype: A Jungian Commentary on the Life of Christ *Edward F. Edinger* ISBN 0-919123-27-9. Illustrated. 144 pp. $15

Personality Types: Jung's Model of Typology
Daryl Sharp ISBN 0-919123-30-9. Diagrams. 128 pp. $14

The Sacred Prostitute: Eternal Aspect of the Feminine
Nancy Qualls-Corbett ISBN 0-919123-31-7. Illustrated. 176 pp. $16

The Survival Papers: Anatomy of a Midlife Crisis
Daryl Sharp ISBN 0-919123-34-1. 160 pp. $15

The Cassandra Complex: Living with Disbelief
Laurie Layton Schapira ISBN 0-919123-35-X. Illustrated. 160 pp. $15

Liberating the Heart: Spirituality and Jungian Psychology
Lawrence W. Jaffe ISBN 0-919123-43-0. 176 pp. $16

The Rainbow Serpent: Bridge to Consciousness
Robert L. Gardner ISBN 0-919123-46-5. Illustrated. 128 pp. $15

Jung Lexicon: A Primer of Terms & Concepts
Daryl Sharp ISBN 0-919123-48-1. Diagrams. 160 pp. $16

Prices and payment (check or money order) in $U.S. (in Canada, $Cdn)
Add Postage/Handling: 1-2 books, $2; 3-4 books, $4; 5-8 books, $7

Complete Catalogue and 36-page SAMPLER free on request

INNER CITY BOOKS, Box 1271, Station Q
Toronto, ON   Canada M4T 2P4   Tel. (416) 927-0355